PRAYER
THE
HIDDEN
FIRE

BOOKS BY TOM HARPUR

Harpur's Heaven and Hell (1983)
For Christ's Sake (1986; reissued 1993)
Always on Sunday (1988)
Life After Death (1991)
God Help Us (1992)
The Uncommon Touch (1994)
Would You Believe? (1996)
Prayer: The Hidden Fire (1998)

TOM HARPUR

PRAYER THE HIDDEN FIRE

A PRACTICAL & PERSONAL APPROACH TO
Awakening a Greater Intimacy with God

Northstone

Editors: Michael Schwartzentruber, Dianne Greenslade
Cover and interior design: Margaret Kyle
Consulting art director: Robert MacDonald

Northstone Publishing acknowledges the financial support of the Government of Canada
through the Book Publishing Industry Development Program for its publishing activities.

Northstone Publishing is an imprint of Wood Lake Books Inc., an employee-owned
company, and is committed to caring for the environment and all creation. Northstone
recycles, reuses, and composts, and encourages readers to do the same. Resources are printed
on recycled paper and more environmentally friendly groundwood papers (newsprint),
whenever possible. The trees used are replaced through donations to the Scoutrees for
Canada program. Ten percent of all profit is donated to charitable organizations.

Canadian Cataloguing in Publication Data
Harpur, Tom
Prayer
Includes bibliographical references and index
ISBN 1–896836–22–4
1. Prayer. I. Title
BV210.2.H37   1998   248.3'2   C98–910466–4

Published by Northstone Publishing,
an imprint of Wood Lake Books Publishing Inc.
Kelowna, British Columbia, Canada

Printing 10 9 8 7 6 5 4 3 2 1
Printed in Canada by
Friesens Printing, Altona, Manitoba

DEDICATION

This is for my mother, Elizabeth Harpur
(née Hoey, Dec.16, 1907–Dec. 2, 1997)
who lived by prayer all her life;
and also for all those who like myself have struggled hard
to live more spiritually and who, nevertheless,
still feel a great need to discover more about praying.

Prayer is the soul's sincere desire
Uttered or unexpressed
The motion of a hidden fire
That trembles in the breast. [1]

James Montgomery, hymnist, 1771–1854.

What Is Prayer? Stanza 1

For with you is the well of life; and in your light
Shall we see light.

Psalm 36:9

Lord of Lords, grant us the good
Whether we pray for it or not.
But evil keep from us,
Even though we pray for it.

Plato (c. 427–348 BCE), Alcibiades, line 1004

CONTENTS

INTRODUCTION

As a deer longs for flowing streams,
So my soul longs for you, O God.

Psalm 42:1

In a moment of prayer, people are at their best,
And whatever their religion, it deserves our respect.

Life magazine, July 1996, in commentary on several large,

beautiful photos of Jews, Muslims, and Buddhists praying

The cover of *Newsweek* magazine for Easter Monday, March 31, 1997, displayed an enormous pair of hands folded in a traditional prayer pose and superimposed on them was the bold headline:

The Mystery Of PRAYER

The stories inside included *Newsweek's* own poll on Americans at prayer. The nationwide survey discovered among several other things that a stunning 87 percent of the population of the United States believe that God answers prayers, 82 percent ask for health or success for a child or other family member when they pray, 75 percent ask for strength to overcome personal weakness, 82 percent say God doesn't play favorites in answering prayer, and 85 percent don't turn away from praying even when their prayers seem to go unanswered. Contrary to what sceptics (who, of course, have their own assumptions, dogmas and beliefs) often maintain, a slim majority of those who believe in prayer (51 percent) don't accept the idea that God answers the prayers of those wanting their team or their athlete to win sporting events. Even so, the poll revealed that the old athletic "Somebody up there likes me" syndrome has much less support among people who are serious about prayer than the media frequently suggest.

Americans today are much more religious, generally speaking, than Canadians and a very large majority of Europeans,

certainly in terms of holding to some regular religious affilia-
tion and to traditional beliefs. Nevertheless, polls in Canada and
elsewhere show surprisingly comparable results when it comes
to the phenomenon of prayer. They reveal that in spite of the
ongoing decline in the membership of institutional religion
throughout the whole of the Western world, the belief in and
the practice of prayer is still shared by a quite overwhelming
majority. For example, none of the hundreds of millions of us
who watched the profoundly moving television coverage of the
funeral of Diana, Princess of Wales, on September 6, 1997, will
ever forget the manner in which people of every age, race, color
and spiritual creed – or absence of one – were all praying in
their own way. As the largest number of human beings ever to
be caught up in a single event (roughly two billion) watched the
ritual in Westminster Abbey and the various processions and
other ceremonies unfold on TV, the world was caught up in a
totally unprecedented, unifying and united outpouring of prayer.
Prayers and tears flowed together around the globe as a universal and instinctual response of the human heart to such tragedy
and deep grief.

What's most significant about the *Newsweek* cover story itself, though, is not so much the intelligent level of the discussion
devoted to prayer and the full gamut of the positive findings
described, it's the fact of the striking prominence given to the
subject itself. The real message of that particular medium was
that prayer is truly of preeminent importance right now. Prayer,
seen as part of the great spiritual awakening going on today –
some would argue it's the most solid part of all – has now become front page news and certainly not just in *Newsweek*. What
is more, having covered religion as a journalist and then as a
regular columnist for Canada's largest newspaper, *The Toronto Star*,

all around the world for more than 25 years (since 1971), I can say with certainty that few, if any, experts in the field would ever have predicted such a development.

Not only that, all kinds of books on prayer, particularly books documenting scientific evidence for "something real" going on, are presently coming to the fore. A noteworthy example of what I'm talking about is Dr. Herbert Benson of Harvard Medical School's bestselling book *Timeless Healing* (1997). His book documents some extraordinary, hard data for the efficacy of meditation – a form of prayer – in the healing of body/mind/spirit. But one could name several books by Larry Dossey, M.D.[1] and a score more. More thoroughly objective experimentation involving faith, prayer and spirituality in general is currently under way in centers all over North America and beyond. The office for the study of complementary medicine at the N.I.H. (National Institute of Health), in Bethesda, Maryland, for example, has several such studies going on at the moment. I have already written of prayer from this perspective in my own investigation of spiritual healing, *The Uncommon Touch* (1994). But the evidence even since then has grown rapidly and in many directions.[2]

Some of the other recent books on prayer take a different tack from the scientific, however. They deal instead with how to use some specific, highly developed tradition of praying, for example, the Spiritual Exercises of St. Ignatius (1491–1556), or some particular and special form of Hindu, Sufi, Buddhist, Jewish, or Christian meditation, often adapted for the more secular majority. But while the scientifically based books are encouraging in one way, and while both the religious and secular books just mentioned undoubtedly have their place for many, a huge gap still cries out to be filled. I have worked as a seminarian, a parish priest (Anglican/Episcopalian), a seminary professor (Greek and New Testament), and spent many years dealing with spiritual and ethical issues as a reporter and a commentator in *The Star* and in various other media, particularly TV. Over all that time, I have yet to read a truly down-to-earth, simple yet honest – from the heart and from the gut – book on prayer.

Indeed, what the following chapters contain is the kind of book on prayer I myself wanted and badly needed many years ago when I first consciously took over my spiritual journey for myself. On this point, I resonate with C. S. Lewis, who taught at Oxford during my years there. He used to say he wrote his children's books – the Narnia tales – in the style of book he had wanted as a child but couldn't find. In other words, like most nonfiction books, certainly those I have personally enjoyed the most, this book is written first of all for the author himself. I felt a need and a desire to set down in full what prayer means to me at this point in my life and where I still have difficulties. In so doing, I have been highly conscious of the fact that I am still far from having "arrived" in prayer myself. This is very much an interim report and sharing from one who is himself a fellow traveler on the same journey.

As such, this book is not intended to answer all possible questions or difficulties about prayer. That would have been a quite unreasonable target to have set in any case. Its ultimate aim is to help both the fully initiated and the bewildered novice – who may not see him- or herself as particularly religious but who may want, nevertheless, to go further and deeper on the spiritual path – to grapple with all the joy and pain of prayer in a fresh way, to think more practically and deeply about this vital and very often "peak" spiritual experience. It is also intended to encourage and, hopefully, to help the reader in her or his own practice of praying.

With that in mind, I have done everything in my power to keep the text as simple, practical, and focused on real life as possible. I have also done my best to be completely honest. Where I don't know, I have said so. Where prayer frustrates, confuses, or at times bores me, I have not attempted any kind of pious cover-up. The subject is too crucial – too sacred in the best sense – for any conscious avoidance of the truth, the whole truth and nothing but the truth. So help me God.

A radio program I once heard on the BBC, during a year of postgraduate study back at Oriel College, Oxford, has echoed in my mind down the years since, particularly when I think about prayer. I was sitting in a room in Nottingham on a lovely spring evening in 1963, having a discussion together with two other budding theologians. All of us were ordained Anglican ministers. One, who was several years older than I, was a former fighter pilot who had become an Anglican priest much later in life. He flew a Spitfire in the Battle of Britain. Suddenly, we became aware that something significant was happening on the radio which was playing in the background. There was an interview in progress with John Robinson, who was the Anglican Bishop of Woolwich, in London. He had just written a small but highly controversial book, *Honest to God*. It was destined to become a major bestseller everywhere.

We quickly gathered around the radio, turned up the volume, and listened avidly. It was all fairly radical theological and ethical thinking for that era – new ways of speaking about God and about a new morality. But what, for me, seemed then to be most radical of all were his comments on prayer. He said that even though he was a bishop and was expected to conform to and uphold traditional church doctrines and practices, he had for a long time not felt comfortable with the Anglican – or indeed any "churchy" – approach to prayer. In fact, he said, he felt very uncomfortable in most of the situations and meetings with his fellow bishops, clergy and laity, where praying or the topic of prayer arose. He added, "I was deeply aware that, whatever trip or train they were on in regard to prayer, I had fallen off long ago." He explained what he meant: that formal prayer, in the Anglican style, and fervent "quiet times" each morning – much championed and faithfully practiced by the evangelical wing of Anglicanism and by keenly Protestant evangelicals in general – did little or nothing for his spiritual life. The three of us felt like cheering. Bound, at least in the letter of church law, to say the formal, daily Offices or services for Morning and Evening Prayer from the *Book of Common Prayer*, as a bare minimum, we knew what he meant. Robinson was speaking to our own sense of the aridity and, on occasions, the futility, of our own "prayer life."

I little dreamed back then that I would one day become a friend of Bishop John Robinson (he soon was universally dubbed "Honest-to-God Robinson"), entertaining him in my home, and discussing his developing ideas with him both there and later in his birthplace, Canterbury, England, during the 1978 Lambeth Conference. He died not all that long ago and his mind and presence are deeply missed by a very large company. What was truly refreshing about him – and indeed about much of the theological ferment of the mid and late 1960s – was his candor, his willingness to question traditional truths and formulas, and his concern to make contact with the real world which many Christians still often ignore but are so fond of saying "God loves." He was a deeply spiritual person as well as a leading New Testament scholar. I'd like to think, and certainly it is my prayer, that in this book you are about to read, his spirit of honesty, his love for God, and his deep desire to communicate with modern men and women, continue to live on.

Two important comments: one about the gender issue with regard to God; the other, concerning the nature of the imagery and names surrounding the God-concept itself.

In my last book (called *Would You Believe?* in Canada and *The Thinking Person's Guide to God* in the United States) I began by saying that, though I totally believe in the beyond-gender nature of the Creator, I have found that trying to avoid the appearance of endorsing patriarchy and theological male chauvinism by using his/her as the personal pronoun can often be awkward and artificial. I announced that for that reason I would use the old, male pronouns throughout. This, however, turned out to be a mistake. Almost immediately I received a number of angry letters from intelligent, articulate women who said my decision had to some degree "spoiled" their reading experience. They said that, disclaimer or not, I had once again inadvertently bolstered the view that God is male. Accordingly, I have chosen to use a variety of styles, so that God will be referred to in what follows as he/she or him/her, as she or he alone (sometimes in close proximity), or as she/he, her/him. My intention, obviously, is not to confuse or to irritate but to make and remake the point that the Divine is above and beyond (transcends) maleness and femaleness alike. God incorporates the essential elements of both while utterly surpassing and transforming them.

The second issue is less patent, perhaps, but all the more important for that. I'm referring to all the rest of our language about a Supreme Being. Whenever any of us thinks, speaks, writes or reads about God, there are certain names and images which instantly come to mind. Some of us think of God as Allah; some as Jehovah (Yahweh); others as Brahman; or as The God and Father of our Lord, Jesus Christ; or as The Great Spirit. The list is virtually endless. God is the reality of a thousand names. The more I study and learn about other faiths the more convinced I am that they have so much more in common when they speak of God than ever appears to be the case at the first superficial glance.

It is also my conviction that the name we use doesn't really matter that much in the end; we are all addressing or describing the same kind of Ultimacy, a final, core Reality far beyond any words to describe. The very moment you or I think that we and our name/definition/creed have cornered the market or said the last word about God, we have actually created an idol – a poor substitute for the Transcendent yet Immanent Source and Sustainer of all things. The one thing prayer reminds us of constantly is the sheer inadequacy of all human thoughts and words to do justice to our ultimate concern: the Ultimate Mind or Intelligence behind and throughout the universe. With this in mind, I have quite deliberately used a wide variety of terms and expressions here for this Higher Power. The aim is to try to widen our consciousness and to offer a deeper basis for unity in our differences. Some of these terms – for example, "The Beyond in our Midst" or "The Ground of all Being" originally used by theologians like Paul Tillich and others and popularized to some degree by John Robinson's book – may not be familiar to all of you but may come to make more sense than more familiar ones. The important thing is to somehow find analogies, metaphors, or traditional religious and spiritual language that make sense to you.

One last matter of importance. Try not to worry too much about your awareness that, from time to time, the picture of God you have in your mind may well be too weak or limited. Our God images need to be constantly expanding, but they're not the key issue here. It's enough to be fully conscious of their limitations and then to move on. For example, I have a very poor and inadequate picture in my mind of what electricity is and of how it operates. This in no ultimate way affects my use and enjoyment of the benefits of this unseen force in my daily life. One can think of a long list of similar realities. The very same is true of prayer.

Finally, here are some preliminary definitions of prayer.

PRAYER AS WAITING UPON GOD

Prayer, like so much in life, often consists mainly of expectant waiting:

Prayer is often only the experience of waiting. Prayer is sometimes nothing more than the conscious experience of desire for God. It might not even be a sense of the presence of God. It might be only darkness and silence.

Dr. Daniel P. Sulmasy, O.F.M., M.D.[3]

At the same time, if we wait in patience, and focus upon God, there is so much more. Here is for me the biblical basis and promise of "waiting upon God" for all who seek the path to personal renewal:

> *The Lord is the everlasting God,*
> *the Creator of the ends of the earth.*
> *He does not faint or grow weary;*

his understanding is unsearchable.
He gives power to the faint,
and strengthens the powerless.
Even youths will faint and be weary,
and the young will fall exhausted;
but those who wait for the Lord
shall renew their strength,
they shall mount up with wings like eagles,
they shall run and not be weary,
they shall walk and not faint.
Isaiah 40:28b–31 [4]

PRAYER AS GOD'S POSSESSION OF ONE'S SOUL

Sister Wendy Beckitt, who is widely known to viewers of the American Public Broadcasting System because of her stunning series on art through the ages, has this to say about the nature of prayer in her book *The Mystery of Love*:

When you set yourself to pray, WHAT DO YOU WANT? If you want God to take possession of you, then you are praying. That is all prayer is. There are no secrets, no shortcuts, no methods. Prayer is the utterly ruthless test of your sincerity. It is the one place in the world where there is nowhere to hide. That is its utter bliss – and its torment. [5]

PART ONE

HOMO ORANS
THE PRAYING
HOMINID

He prayeth best who loveth best
All things both great and small;
For the dear God who loveth us,
He made and loveth all.

Samuel Taylor Coleridge, 1772–1834

The Ancient Mariner (1798) Part VII, Stanza 23

I

WHY PRAY?

The wish for prayer is a prayer in itself.
George Bernanos, *Diary of a Country Priest*, 1936

———

Send me the love that keeps the heart still
with the fullness of peace.
Rabindranath Tagore, 1861–1941

———

O Great Spirit, help me always to speak the truth quietly,
To listen with open mind when others speak,
And to remember the peace that may be found in silence.
Ancient Cherokee prayer

When they begin to think seriously about prayer, the question which pops up first in many people's minds is this:"Why bother to pray at all?" I am not talking here about atheists or about those who see themselves as the enemies or mockers of faith or religious practices, for whatever reasons. I am talking about average, well-meaning, well-disposed-towards-a-spiritual-path people whose thinking runs something like this: Supposing God exists and that this God is both loving and all-knowing, why would such a God or Cosmic Intelligence require his/her "children" to keep calling out, asking for things, listing their problems, or going on about how great he/she is, when all of this would not be "news" or hidden from the Deity's "sight" in any case?

I suppose the shortest, most honest and accurate reply to this is,"God alone knows." But clearly that doesn't get us where we want to be. Belief that requires a rational underpinning, a holistic approach from both sides of the brain, has to have something more satisfying than that to go on. Paradoxical though it seems, the Christian gospels and most of the world's other sacred texts comfortably hold together both poles of this discussion. They make it clear that God does indeed know our needs and petitions before we ask, yet they insist repeatedly on the urgent need for us to pray and to tell God what obviously God alone already knows more fully than we can ever hope to articulate.

All religions hold a startlingly similar view of prayer and we may have real differences with any or all of them. Still, we know it would be very foolish to assume blithely that there's not some deep reason of the heart for the apparent contradiction involved here. For that reason I am quite sure that, paradoxical or not, something truly important for the human condition is being said. Such a belief is reinforced by the fact that, since recorded time began, human beings everywhere have had prayer as an integral, indeed central, part of their relationship with the Mystery under, behind, and through all that is. Our species, as I have said more than once in my newspaper writing, could well be described not as Homo Sapiens – an intelligent hominid – but as Homo Orans; in other words, as a praying hominid. We are animals and belong intricately to all living creatures and the entire biosystem of the planet. But, as far as we can know, other animals do not pray. Speaking generally, however, prayer comes as naturally to human hearts and lips as breathing itself.

I've puzzled over this conundrum of why we feel and are told by the founders of the great world religions that we need to pray, when the kind of God most of them go on to describe surely already knows what is in the depths of our minds and hearts. The insight which has always helped me most is this: that one of the things God knows about us is our deeply human need, as intelligent creatures, to pray or to communicate with the Ultimate, with God. What verifies this in my own experience is the natural, at times almost inexorable, yearning or urgency within my own soul, in my innermost being, leading me to prayer. Try to neglect or ignore it as I may, through laziness, self-assurance, or dryness of soul, it wells up. It may be just a quick, "Thank you," or it may be an emotional, lengthy outpouring of angst or need. Even while I'm aware that he knows all that's going on in my life or the lives of those around me, I am compelled to converse with the Great Spirit, or, by just being still, to listen for the Divine Voice within.

I intuitively know for certain that this would remain true whether I ever become so disillusioned with formal, institutionalized worship that I gave it up entirely or not. The option of leaving Anglicanism (Episcopalianism) – perhaps to join the Quakers – is far from being impossible. My wife, Susan, and I have tried over the years to continue in our adherence to this or that form of parish worship yet find that the dogmatic rigidities pervading it all overwhelm and hinder any spirituality that makes sense to us. We make no judgment of those who still find them relevant and full of meaning. Honesty, however, compels me to say that for us worship and especially prayer in such restrictive circumstances often seem more like a repetitive exploration of an ancient archeological dig than the expression of a living encounter with divine reality today. But that is another story.

Where does this deep compulsion itself – what the noted hymnwriter James Montgomery called "a hidden fire" within – originate? Sceptics will tell you it's all part of our alleged childish need for a champion or parent "in the sky," an attempted denial of the putative "fact" that we are "on our own in the universe," or as the late Carl Sagan used to put it, alone "on this pale blue dot" called Earth. I have attempted to deal with the true reasons for belief in God and with the arguments of those who deny there is a Supreme Being or Presence elsewhere and so do not intend to repeat that effort here.[1] Instead, assuming that our urge, need, and sometimes well-nigh inexpressible longing to cry out to God arises from an inner, intuitive, and near-universal certainty that there *is* a Divine Source, an Author/Creator of all the vast reaches of the cosmos (the Greek word, *Kosmos*, means a place of order, purpose and design), it seems to me eminently reasonable that this Fount of all Reality doesn't just know of our need to pray but has actually designed us specifically that we might come to know and be more like her by this means. We are, as Harvard's Herbert Benson, M.D. says, "wired for God."[2] This is part of the meaning of the Genesis account in which humans are described as "made in the image of God." We have been created for a purpose, to know, love, and serve the Great Spirit, or the Beyond in our Midst, the Author and Sustainer of all being, both animate and inanimate. The Creator is a communicating Source and wills us to develop an intimate fellowship with herself.

A series of quotes from sacred writings and other evidence of all kinds from all ages could quickly illustrate that the most diverse of religious traditions, tribes, and "tongues" and cultures of every kind still hold this belief. Even the first known paintings in the history of art, those 20,000-year-old, awe-inspiring creatures depicted on the walls and roof of the Lascaux Cave in the Dordogne region of France, may have been a form of prayer.

It is important, though, to point out that in order to know and to grow like someone we admire and love, in order to understand their motives and their real intentions towards us – as we progress on to become friends or even lovers – we need to spend time together both in silence and in the most intimate kind of discourse. Prayer, which has often been described as a "conversation with God," has precisely this object in view. God – in addition to knowing what we need before we ask; in addition to knowing our great need to express our deepest doubts, hopes, fears, feelings of sadness and of celebration, our most urgent concerns for others – knows he/she has designed us for a deep, and eventually a never-to-be-disrupted friendship, partnership and intimacy with himself/herself. As St. Augustine once said, "You have made us for yourself; and our hearts are restless until they find their rest in you." Prayer, then, is a deep soul conversation with the Divine, an intimacy with Ultimacy for which we were designed from the very beginning.

But remember too that there is an intensely communal aspect to this intimate partnership or sharing with the Divine. While I plan mainly to discuss here the prayer life of the individual, I do so in the awareness that prayer in a community – be it only two or three others or a vast assembly – is also part of God's plan for our spiritual fulfillment as a species. If you haven't got a regular place where you can share in prayer with others or have never looked for one, you can make your own. Initially, all that is necessary is to find one or two others who share your desire and to agree on a regular time and place to meet. There is much mutual encouragement in this as well as more power.

BUT IS IT ALWAYS ANSWERED?

I have covenanted in the introduction to be truthful and real, so I want to be as direct and honest here as I can be. The above arguments all carry a lot of weight with me. However, they only provide a partial answer to the original question, "Why pray?" Let me say frankly that what motivates me most to pray and what keeps me at it even though at times of bleakness my prayers may seem to get "no farther than the ceiling" is that I have discovered I have no other choice. I have been consciously struggling with praying for almost half a century – through good times and bad, through successes and failures, through times of great weakness or of sadness and depression as well as those long periods of many months, and often years, when everything seemed full of energy, well-being and achievement. My own experience confirms what millions of church members and the vast company of the faithful in other world religions also testify to: prayer makes a tremendous difference in one's life.

Once again, I don't need to bring forward a "great cloud of witnesses." Quite honestly, one could fill many books by simply collecting anthologies of such testimonies given by both ordinary people and by the distinguished and famous of every age and generation. As a species, we have decided to stick with praying because we have found that prayer works and most of us – certainly this has proven true for me – cannot function either well or long without it. Prayer is never left unanswered even though the specific response can very often be an apparent "no" or may seem like no response at all at the time. Very frequently, my prayers have seemingly been ignored, having fallen upon apparently "deaf ears." Ambiguities abound. There have often been long periods of soul "dryness," when the experience of what the Psalms so often describe as "God's absence" or "God's hiddenness" have seemed to lord it over any other. Yet while granting all of this, there has been, and still remains within, the solid conviction that something deeply meaningful and solid has been going on all the time.

I am, for example, genuinely amazed at how often in the course of my life what was to me at the actual moment it was going on a source of immense frustration – an apparently total failure of prayer to achieve anything – has so often been proven to have been the very best "answer" I could have had. I mean this in all sincerity and seriousness. There is so much wisdom in the folk saying, "Be careful what you pray for; you could get it." Looking back, I now realize that the outcome I so desperately sought at one time or another – fully convinced that because it was my will, or perhaps my father's or someone else's close to my life, it must surely also be God's will – would have been a complete disaster. Getting my way, or having my prayers "answered" on my terms at that point (that is, having the main thrust of my petitions granted), would undoubtedly have been a huge step in the wrong direction, indeed possibly even a direct tragedy. The more I reflect on my life – and I challenge the reader to do the same – the more I can discern a wisdom and design at work that has been and continues to be far beyond my own.

In this respect, the astoundingly popular book *The Celestine Prophecy*, by James Redfield, is correct. The amazing synchronicities in our lives are by design, not accident. They reveal an intelligence and spirit at work much surpassing our own.³ This wisdom has been most evident for me *in retrospect* when the expected or hoped-for answer to my prayers has completely failed to materialize and something quite different has turned up instead. The more you read spiritual literature and sacred texts the more universally this experience can be corroborated. The Apostle Paul found it to be so in his own life and testifies to it in a number of his letters, but especially in the Letter to the Romans where he proclaims that all things "work together for good" for those who love God (Romans 8:28). This is not based upon some abstract theorizing or the experience of an academic who has spent his life in the peaceful shelter of ivy-covered walls at a college or university. Paul knew terrible dangers, crises, and suffering himself – coming both from without and from within.

Tulku Thondup, a Tibetan Buddhist who has written a number of books on the relevance of Buddhist ideas to western life, says in his latest work, *The Healing Power of Mind*, "In many ways, the great tragedies of my life turned out to be blessings..."⁴ A letter from a patient to the great psychoanalyst Carl Jung, sent to me long ago by a reader of my columns and which I have kept close at hand ever since, begins with the words, "Looking back on my life, I can see how out of (apparent) evil much good has come..."

Nevertheless, in spite of what I have just said above, it's still obviously true that not everything can be put in neat, satisfying categories or readily explained. I have often prayed with parents at the hospital bedside of an infant or a child who was ill or who had been severely injured in an accident and our urgent prayers were not "answered." The baby or youngster died. In the past, when I functioned as an official Anglican minister, first in a parish and then teaching young seminarians, I have conducted funeral services for teenagers, for young parents – for all "sorts and conditions of men" and women – more times than I care to remember. For the most part, these were all people for whom much prayer had been offered. Great good has indeed often eventually followed such genuine tragedies – healing of family relationships, a waking up of relatives or friends who were perhaps walking unconsciously through life never realizing the temporary nature of everything, the setting up of charities or of trust funds for children or adults afflicted with terminal diseases. Many of those most closely affected by such occasions for sorrow become more compassionate light-bearers or helpers to others. But just as often, it seems, the negative "answer" in such cases has caused such grief or bitterness that marriages have broken up, or those concerned have become haunted by depression and bitter anger towards God. It is certainly hard, even sometimes quite impossible, to see the bigger picture in a great many of life's tragedies. I don't profess to have any smooth explanations. There are none, though many pious religionists feel they must always have them at the ready, together with some apt scriptural passage.

Still, the opportunity for spiritual growth in such apparent failures of prayer is often missed. I do not personally believe that such tragedies are "sent" to us by God for that purpose – to edify, punish or warn us. But it is remarkable how quite similar people, reacting to almost exactly the same crisis of faith, can do so in such completely opposite ways. It is anything but predetermined. Our own choice is clearly involved. You can actually see it happening from outside in the case of others. The old aphorism may seem a cliché but it's still true: The same water that wears away stone can also harden steel. This really is not so much a failure of prayer, something to be blamed on God (indeed death itself can often be understood as a form of healing) but a failure by some, in fact by all of us at one time or another, to wrestle with an admittedly sorely tested faith until we win at least some kind of spiritual victory. I will return to that theme in a later chapter.

A FAMILIAR "PRAYER" THROWS LIGHT ON THE ISSUE

In my own life, while I have often been puzzled and perplexed by the apparent strangeness of God's ways toward myself and the rest of humanity, I have also discovered that the promise of Psalm 23 has, in the end, always been fulfilled. The psalm begins with the healing words, "The Lord is my shepherd, I shall not want..." and goes on to say, "Even though I walk through the darkest valley, I will fear no evil; for you are with me." One is drawn closer in renewed intimacy, and the depth of the conversation becomes more honest and clear, when the shadows of the valley begin to cast their shade over one's life. That pain often leads to deeper prayer is a widely observable phenomenon. It is what caused Kahlil Gibran (1883–1931), in his long poem *The Prophet*, to write, "You pray in your distress and in your need; would that you might pray also in the fullness of your joy and in your days of abundance."

Speaking of Psalm 23, the reason for its imperishable vitality and relevance in Western spirituality lies in its quiet profundity and at the same time in its simplicity. It is not in the form of a traditional prayer – or rather, it is a highly moving prayer, but one not of asking but of confident affirmation. No matter what your faith or lack thereof, if you have never done so before, I urge you to experiment with affirming this "prayer" daily for a month. I'll be most surprised if you don't decide to make it part of the core of your spiritual life from now on.

Perhaps, though, its very familiarity has dulled both the freshness of its initial impression and its deeper meaning for us. That's why I want to look at it again just briefly. Although more recent translations can no doubt help to enable one to see it with renewed freshness, here it is in the much more traditional – and eloquent – King James Version of 1611:

> *The Lord is my shepherd;*
> *I shall not want.*
> *He maketh me to lie down in green pastures:*
> *He leadeth me beside the still waters.*
> *He restoreth my soul:*
> *he leadeth me in the paths of righteousness*
> *for his name's sake.*
> *Yea, though I walk through*
> *the valley of the shadow of death,*
> *I will fear no evil:*
> *for thou art with me;*
> *thy rod and thy staff they comfort me.*

Thou preparest a table before me
in the presence of my enemies:
thou anointest my head with oil;
my cup runneth over.
Surely goodness and mercy shall
follow me all the days of my life:
and I will dwell in the house of the Lord
for ever.

I won't comment on all of this soaring prayer/affirmation here.
There are a few things to keep in mind, however, when making
it more deeply your own.

First, a note about the metaphor with which the psalm begins:
God as shepherd, human beings as the sheep. Unfortunately,
overly sweet, stained-glass representations and other pictures in
words have misinterpreted this imagery for many centuries and
have missed the point. In antiquity, the shepherd metaphor was
the highest symbol or imagery for virile leadership, for strength
and farsightedness. Vigorous, righteous kings were often described
as true shepherds of the people. For the Greeks of the classical
era, mighty Agamemnon was the shepherd of his people. It had
nothing to do with pale, effete-looking persons with a saintly
smile firmly in place. Neither had it anything to do with fluffy,
white, fairy-tale sheep when illustrating our human relationship
to the Divine. Having once worked on a sheep farm in the
English Cotswolds during my student days, I can verify not only
that sheep are indeed remarkably silly and extremely wayward,
they also stink. They are prone to innumerable illnesses, some of
them quite disgusting in nature. In other words, they're anything but idyllic creatures, however cute they may look from
the distance of a passing train or car. We need to cut through all

the habitual sweetness and light surrounding them if we are to grasp the real message here.

Second, if you're in a hurry some day, and yet want to catch once more the essence of this psalm, the first line really says it all, in my view. The statement, "I shall not want" is based on a deep understanding of what it truly means to say that the Creator of the universe cares about you in a personal way. It means that, in spite of many hard and strange vicissitudes and the way things may seem to us, in the final denouement, God has promised that we shall never be in dire need of whatever it is that is truly essential to our ultimate happiness in this world and the next. As the Buddha pointed out, the true cause of suffering in the world is the host of our desires, our graspings, our wants. Like Christ, he taught that if the lower ego with its "grasping at" or "attachment to" physical realities can be restrained or "crucified," much of the inevitable suffering can be avoided or reduced greatly. To say, "I shall not want," then, clearly doesn't mean every petty wish or ephemeral desire will be granted. It means instead that nothing essential to our survival, our final peace or happiness (within the timing and will of God) will ever be lacking in this life or beyond.

There is so much more one could say. But the last aspect I want to draw your attention to is one which I haven't seen in any of the many commentaries on Psalm 23, though undoubtedly others must have noticed it too. Specifically, it is only when the author comes to the valley of the shadow (the *New Revised Standard Version* translates the lines as: "Even though I walk through the darkest valley, I fear no evil; for you are with me.") that he changes from talking about God in the third person "he" and reverts to the incredibly more intimate second person, "thou." This bears out what I have already said about the way difficult times in our lives often end up provoking more intimacy in praying, if we let them.

THE EXAMPLE OF CHRIST

People of other faiths can learn much from Christ's own deep experience of prayer: his inexorable need to pray in the Garden of Gethsemane before his arrest and crucifixion; his highly emotional petition to God to "let this cup [of suffering] pass from me"; the resounding "no" which was his answer and which was made infinitely worse by his sense of God-forsakenness as he hung on the cross.

Whatever your Christology (your rational understanding of who Jesus was) may be, few spiritually minded people would deny that Christ felt, in his innermost being, a profound and perhaps unique sense of oneness with the Divine. His trust in God and his deep prayer life cannot be questioned. The gospels make both abundantly clear. Yet he, too, knew what it was like to have his prayers "answered" quite differently from what, as a full human being, he so earnestly desired. He still prayed on, though, even while feeling abandoned, on the cross itself. Easter, for Christians, was God's answer.

CONCLUSION

Finally, though I already hinted at it much earlier, I would answer the sceptic's query, "Why pray?" quite simply by saying that most of the time, facing life's joys and dilemmas, I simply haven't had the foggiest notion of how else to respond, or of what else to do. I don't like to think of prayer as a last resort, as a "turn to prayer in foxholes once the shooting starts" type of approach. But, honestly and practically, that's how it is.

I remember driving a small English-made car (a Morris Minor) up through the Haliburton Highlands of southern Ontario one time, many years ago. It was early June and the tightly winding Highway 35 was wet in some spots and still extremely rough in others from the winter's frost having broken it up as it thawed. As we headed down into a particularly acute curve, the combination of water on the road, a corrugated surface, and the turn itself resulted in the car spinning completely out of control. As it skidded and bucked, there wasn't a thing I could do. It all seemed to be happening in a time warp or in slow motion. I felt really alert and sharply focused or concentrated because of the adrenalin rush, but at the same time quite powerless. Immediately, I found myself silently praying with urgent conviction. After what seemed like an eternity but was actually only a matter of several seconds, the car flipped over completely and came to rest against a huge rock at the bottom of the decline and beyond the small ditch on the opposite side of the road. One suitcase had been flung out of the car and smashed to pieces. But, apart from a few bruises and being badly tossed around, my passenger and I remained unhurt. The car was beyond repair.

In the course of my life, this kind of intense prayer has often happened quite involuntarily. It was the only resort left at the time and some kind of survival instinct promptly called it up. What's more, I know that most readers of this book have had similar experiences. Indeed one of the values of a regular prayer life, however untraditional, is that when such emergencies come it is almost always our first, intuitive response. As a carefully honed tool it's instantly at the ready when chaos, panic or great danger break out. As clergy of all faiths are fond of noting, with a nod to Alfred, Lord Tennyson, more things have been "wrought by prayer" at times like these than many would even care to admit.

In his important 1994 book on meditation, *Wherever You Go, There You Are*, Dr. Jon Kabat-Zinn tells the story of how Mohandas Gandhi met his death at the hands of a gun-toting assassin.[5] Instantly upon being mortally shot, Gandhi looked directly at his killer, put his hands together in the form of a tent at his heart, in the typically Hindu gesture of acknowledging the divine in everyone, and died with his favorite prayer or mantra on his lips. He had so accustomed himself to constant prayer and compassion for all that he was able to meet death with the same equanimity and generosity of spirit he practiced throughout his entire life. One reason for praying "without ceasing" (1 Thessalonians 5:17) is that when you are looking a crisis immediately "in-the-face," the time for rationalizing or for philosophizing has long passed and the urge to pray has become automatic.

A POSTSCRIPT: HOW DOES PRAYER WORK?

Quite truthfully, I do not know how prayer works. Nor do I believe anyone else knows with absolute certainty. Obviously, though, it is a question of ongoing importance and concern. At the moment, as I noted in the introduction, there are numerous scientifically designed tests being undertaken at a number of centers in the United States and in Europe.[6] Already some early results seem to support my own contention here – as well as the widespread, popular conviction – that good things begin to happen when you pray. There is a very long way to go, however, before the actual "mechanism" or process at work in prayer is fully explained. In a way, the problem here is akin to that involved in spiritual and other complementary healing approaches of various kinds. Those who know it most intimately are absolutely sure that such healing does work. However, when it comes to explaining how it functions, the answers are many and still scientifically vague, in spite of some very hopeful clues. (Conventional medicine, of course, has the same problem with a vast array of mysteries.) Most sceptics regarding prayer, therefore, insist that like it or not, prayer is really a form of talking to yourself. If it does any good at all, it does it to you, the person praying, and to nobody else – a form of self-help or self-hypnosis.

I was strongly reminded of this kind of criticism in a restaurant recently. Three of us, my wife, her father and I, were having lunch in the cafeteria of Eaton's, one of Toronto's largest department stores. Gradually, I became aware of a woman's voice carrying on an earnest conversation just behind me. I turned as casually as I could for a look because there was such an intrusive flow of words, without interruption or answer from anybody else, that it seemed just a little odd. The woman speaking looked perfectly normal – middle-aged, well-dressed, and quite rational-sounding. But she was totally oblivious of everyone else as she talked away to some invisible partner or friends.

Yet, while it perhaps has a fleeting superficial appeal to non-believers in prayer, this analogy or explanation fails to account for the inner knowledge of the millions who pray today or who have testified eloquently to their experience of praying in past years. Everybody knows what it feels like to talk to oneself and there are times when it can be very useful. As an old Scot once said, "I talk to myself now and then for two principal reasons – I like to hear a sound man talk, and I certainly like to talk to a sound man!" But praying is markedly different from this and the one doing the praying knows it. In genuine prayer there is a communion or sharing going on that makes one aware of another level or order of reality altogether. Not always, but often enough to be unforgettable, one is conscious of being touched by, or of reaching out and touching for oneself, the fringes of the robe of God. What happens is sometimes ineffable; it can't be put into words, but its deep reality is *more* rather than *less* because of that fact.

Still, how does it work? It's not a matter of persuading God to do something she is reluctant to do. It's not a bargaining, though we often are tempted to make it such, where we promise to be different in very specific ways if only this or that favor is granted. Supremely, it is a matter of our obedience both to divine command and to our own inner need, particularly when we pray – not fatalistically or fearfully – that God's will be done in all things. In *The Uncommon Touch*, I suggested that the final answer to how prayer works will be found in the realm of subtle energies and of consciousness studies. I believe that prayer is an attempt to align oneself or one's community with the cosmic will of the Supreme Intelligence; that it projects subtle information – light and healing energy – towards the one or the many being prayed for. Ultimately, all being, animate and inanimate, is held and enfolded by various kinds of consciousness and information. Prayer, I believe, taps into that and releases it in our own lives and those of the ones for whom we pray.

Is this in some way unfair? Does God play favorites? Plainly not. This resource exists for all to find and use. It is limitless and present everywhere, like God herself.

I hope one day there will be better explanations or more scientific ones than I have offered here. Meanwhile, the invitation is to put prayer to the test in one's own life and see the difference. You don't have to understand how a car or a computer works to use them and find them effective. I'm living proof of that every day of my life! To borrow a term the late

Canadian novelist Robertson Davies once used to describe himself in an interview with me, I too am a "techno-moron." But I get by. The same, of course, is true of so much more in the universe around us. Few really could explain how gravity works. They have never seen it or touched it. They nevertheless know it works, from its influence and results all around us. I have written this elsewhere but it's an extremely important truth to keep in mind when discussing things spiritual. Even when it comes to understanding such familiar-seeming realities as matter itself, most people are considerably more vague. Scientists themselves are now forced to use symbols and analogies in discussing it. Matter is not so much a "stuff" as a "wave" or "dance of energy," they say. In the final analysis, the spiritual path, particularly the way of prayer, is an experience rather than a theory. As the psalmist once said, "O taste and see that the Lord is good..." (Psalm 34:8).

SOMETHING PRACTICAL TO WORK ON

Take time to experiment. As suggested earlier, why not take Psalm 23 – or if you prefer, some other brief passage from the world's sacred or inspirational literature – and work with it daily for a month. Pray it or affirm it as your own prayer, adapting it where necessary. "Taste and see" for yourself what a difference it can make.

II

A CASE STUDY

I waited patiently for the Lord;
he inclined unto me and heard my cry.
He drew me up from the desolate pit,
out of the miry bog,
and set my feet upon a rock,
making my steps secure.
He put a new song in my mouth,
a song of praise to our God.
Many will see and fear,
and put their trust in the Lord.

Psalm 40:1–3

I promised that this treatment of prayer would be personal and practical rather than pious or theoretical. Here is an example, from my own experience in praying, of getting what seemed to be a wrong, evil, or "non-answer," from an immediate point of view, and then in time of coming to realize that the "right" answer was there all the time – an answer that was a lot richer and more meaningful for my own growth than anything I originally had in mind.

The story has to do with health, something most of us pray for daily almost as a matter of course. Over a period of several days early in 1997, I wrote the following account (in my own abbreviated code) in my journal.

———

Looking back, 1996 was in many ways both "the best of times" and "the worst of times," to borrow Charles Dickens' famous words. Many good things were happening. My book *Would You Believe? Finding God Without Losing Your Mind* was published in the spring and I did the customary publicity tour across Canada, with appearances on CBC Radio's *Morningside* and on most of the other media outlets coveted by publishers and authors alike. The majority of reviews were positive and the book was on the nonfiction bestsellers list in the *Globe and Mail*, "Canada's National Newspaper," for about 12 weeks.

By September of that year, an American publisher, Prima Press, in California, had bought the U.S. rights and had brought out their own hardcover version of the book with the title *The Thinking Person's Guide to God – Overcoming the Obstacles to Belief.* Up to this point I had had little success in making much of an incursion into that large and important market.

Later in the fall of 1996, my earlier book, *Life After Death* (1991), was televised in a ten-part Canadian series which I hosted on Vision/TV, the world's first interfaith TV network. It ran in prime time from Monday to Friday for two weeks, was repeated Tuesday nights for ten weeks, and received the largest audience Vision had ever had for a Canadian documentary production.[1] City TV, also based in Toronto, then ran the series in Ontario and on some of its other affiliates across Canada. A Quebec producer made a French version and an edited, two-hour presentation of the English show ran on U.S. television on The Learning Channel. Prospects for more foreign exposure were looking good. McClelland and Stewart, my publisher at the time, had brought out a mass paperback edition of the book, with a new cover, to coincide with the television launch and there were large posters of the cover in bookstores everywhere. While part of me enjoyed the increased recognition and meeting viewers, I nevertheless soon began to discover the down side of even such minor celebrity. You tend to take personal privacy for granted until you begin to lose it.

But, that apart, there was indeed much for which to be extremely thankful and my prayer life reflected that. Incidentally, the weekly, syndicated ethics/spirituality column in *The Sunday Star*, which I had been writing for about 12 years, was flowing more easily than ever before and reader response was steadily increasing. The other side, of course, was that it took much more time and effort to answer the otherwise welcome growing spate of mail.[2]

I cite all of this not in an attempt to parade or flaunt supposed "achievements" but to contrast the way in which at the same time, alongside these and all the quite mundane things that make up the ordinary but meaningful fabric of anyone's life, another story was unfolding.

It had come to my attention for the first time early in January 1996, and the account should be prefaced by two observations. The first is that my habit for some years now has been to take a five-mile (eight-kilometer) walk every morning on weekdays before getting down to work at my desk. While I have three or four favorites, my most frequent path follows a beautiful country sideroad north of Toronto. It runs over a corner of the greater Toronto area's "mink and manure belt" – a region of hilly, forested uplands and farms, near King City, on a vast glacial deposit known as the Oak Ridges Moraine. The little kettle lake nearby on which we live owes its formation some 14,000 years ago to the same Ice Age phenomena that produced the moraine. I always use this hiking time for meditation, prayer, and a lot of mental "free-floating." Most of my better ideas seem to come out of this leisurely, even rather casual process. The second relevant point is that out of one of the coldest winters for many years, the weather in early January 1996 was by far the most severe I have ever encountered outside of trips as a journalist to the high Arctic.

I had parked my car on the edge of the road as usual one day and headed west into a bitter wind. At first, the sideroad I follow dips a little before rising sharply into the first big hill. I found it much tougher going than usual. The sunshine was brilliant and the branches of the bare trees were finely etched against the pale blue sky. Fields where sheep and cattle often graze in summer lay wrapped in shining snow and silence. But it was so cold it was difficult to breathe and the wind stung the small amount of skin showing between my beard and my well-pulled-down cap. Halfway up the stiffening climb, I suddenly began to feel an unpleasant sensation in my lungs – as if sandpaper had touched lightly on raw flesh. It wasn't painful, exactly. It was

more of a moderate discomfort. My first thought was that perhaps in the extreme cold I had somehow "burned" my lungs
with frost.

I continued walking at the same pace, however, stopping
only to pull my scarf up over my mouth and nose. The strange
sensation, just under my breastbone and fairly high up in my
chest, remained about the same for seven or eight minutes
and then, as I left the incline behind, it gradually dissipated.
The rest of the walk, while involving even steeper hills at
times, was uneventful, free from unpleasant feelings of any
kind. I thought no more about it. I even continued my regular habit of enjoying one or two pipefuls of my favorite tobacco, Green Sail, as I walked. Of course, I never inhaled –
intentionally at any rate.

However, the next day and for the rest of the week I had
precisely the same experience at the same point in the walk and
for approximately the same length of time. When I worked out
on a treadmill at home one day instead of taking on a genuine
blizzard outdoors, the odd chest feeling never showed up. This
seemed to indicate that my first instinct had been right; I must
have inadvertently got a case of frostbite in my bronchial tubes.
I was sure that eventually it would heal and go away. The problem was that it didn't.

Prayer seemed to have no effect whatever. In fact, I was
finding it quite difficult to pray about it. My mind was con-
flicted between taking it seriously and hoping that if I ignored
it, it would go away. I even found myself praying at times, "God,
if it's anything at all, please heal it. If it isn't, help me get rid of
my stupid phobias around it."

Even though I had lots of energy and could climb stairs, do
chores and so forth without sensations of any kind, I was grow-

ing concerned. So was Susan. After several weeks, I went reluctantly to my family doctor and told him about my walking in the freezing weather and how I thought I had perhaps slightly frozen part of my lungs. He looked me over thoroughly and said that although everything seemed normal he thought I should see a cardiologist and undergo a thallium stress test just to make sure the sensation wasn't a form of angina.

I was surprised and somewhat annoyed. Couldn't the man hear? There I was, telling him it was a self-induced bronchial difficulty, and how generally fit I felt – I have been an avid walker, swimmer and canoeist ever since I grew too old for the team sports of rowing, rugger and basketball – and he was sitting there suggesting I might have a cardiac problem. Embarrassing as it is to describe, I felt insulted. Nevertheless, when he insisted on making an appointment for me with a specialist, I agreed to go for an initial consultation.

The youngish cardiologist was kindly in his overall manner even though he projected a certain detached or clinical aura common to many in his profession. He heard my story, did a quick physical examination, found nothing amiss, and then rather too automatically, I thought, called his secretary to book a stress test for me at the hospital in two weeks.

Knowing that it's no use praying and then not doing whatever one can do for oneself, I felt compelled to go along with the arrangement. I was quite apprehensive, however, about the test. In spite of feeling well and fit, I wondered how long they would keep the exercise machine going. Would they force me to go beyond a reasonable level of exertion in an attempt to find – or even to make – a problem? Was there a risk of creating trouble when there was nothing "broken" and therefore nothing that required "fixing"?

When the day came, I put my concerns and questions to the male technician in charge of the preliminaries. He said there was nothing to worry about since the cardiologist himself would be on hand to cope with any emergency! Somehow this well-meant assurance only served to alarm me further. I recalled an ancient prayer: "Lord, please save me from people who mean well."

At a deeper level, however, I was praying that best-known of all personal prayer-complaints: "Yes, I know this kind of thing can happen to other people, Lord, but why me? Why now?" Next, I started another familiar human twist or evasion – bargaining with God: "I'll stop smoking so much – no, I'll stop smoking the pipe altogether if this all goes away soon. Anything, Lord, just don't let me have heart problems." Juvenile? Yes. But I was surprised at how easily these thoughts flowed.

By the time my chest had been shaved, all the various electrodes had been attached to my upper body, and I'd had time to take in the different screens, machines and other electronic wizardry in the lab where the test was to be done, I felt even more dubious about the affair. It really came as a distracting relief to feel the treadmill starting to move. I tried to absorb the atmosphere of the piny woods depicted on a huge wall poster directly in front of me as the device began to speed up and to tilt upwards more and more. It was like walking or nearly jogging up a major hill. Simultaneously, a nurse standing beside me had begun to inject a substance into my bloodstream which would later show up on the scanner and indicate the amount of blood flow to the heart while under extended exercise stress.

After several minutes, during which my overall feeling was good in spite of some anxiety, the nurse began asking me how I

was. "Are you okay?" she repeatedly intoned. At the same moment, out of the corner of my eye I could see the doctor with
some animation occasionally pointing to something on one of
the screens and commenting on it to the technician beside him.
There seemed to be a gradual change in the mood of the room.
I felt a slight stab of panic. This served to make it harder to
breathe and so my fears increased. At around the nine-minute
mark I decided I had had enough and said so.

The technician promptly removed all the wires and, without comment from anyone, I was led off into an adjoining room
for the scan. As we walked, I asked the young man if there had
been some problem. He mumbled something about possible
left ventricular "irregularities," but when I tried to press him he
said I'd have to wait to see what the scan showed and what the
doctor had to say about it. Although in my mind I had gone
back to bargaining prayers, the scan itself proved harmless enough
and I was shortly on my way home.

Though I remained certain that there was nothing wrong,
Susan and I spent anxious days over the next two weeks waiting
for my next appointment with the specialist and whatever news
it might bring. This is an experience many of you know only
too well. It seemed an interminably long delay before hearing
the results, but we reminded ourselves of how many thousands
of others were going through this kind of ordeal and much
worse in medical clinics and hospitals all the time.

Eventually, the day came and I went for our meeting. The
doctor was polite but at the same time fairly curt. The test, he
said, showed ominous signs. He interpreted these signs as in-
dicative of a major blockage in one of the three key coronary
arteries, specifically the left anterior descending artery (the LAD)
which supplies blood to the crucial left ventricle and the apex

of the heart where heart rhythms are determined and regulated. As I sat feeling slightly stunned, he said I should undergo an angiogram as soon as one could be booked in order to determine the extent and full nature of the presumed blockage. He called his secretary to have this set up and then presented me with a prescription for coated aspirin, a beta-blocker, and a nitroglycerin sprayer to carry at all times. It was so unexpected that I found it hard to take it all in let alone pray even so much as an "arrow prayer." I queried him about the risks of an angiogram because I had heard somewhere that strokes or heart attacks can be triggered by this invasive technology. "Yes," he said, "there's some risk. But the odds against anything going wrong are about 400 to one. You'll be fine."

The next thing I knew I was out in the warm spring sunshine feeling more than a little shocked and upset and wondering what was really happening to me. Basically, I was convinced there must be some mistake. I put the date for the angiogram in my daybook but, to be honest, I had no intention of going through with it. I postponed it once and then later cancelled it completely. I stopped taking both the aspirin and the blocker almost immediately in the ongoing, deep belief that it was a breathing problem and would soon disappear.

Susan believed my assertions that I felt well and as vigorous as ever; however, she worried about the possibility of denial on my part and the deep uncertainty we were now left in by my refusing to proceed with the angiogram. At her encouragement, I read Dr. Dean Ornish's 1990 *New York Times* bestseller *Reversing Heart Disease*. We decided to commit ourselves to his "prevention diet," which is a strictly vegetarian, low-fat regime, combined with yoga and progressive relaxation. It's somewhat less rigorous than the Ornish "reversal diet" in which the amount of calories gained from fat are restricted to a bare minimum.[3]

I also resolved to stop smoking – something I had done continuously ever since college days in England nearly 40 years ago. On June 3, 1996, we made a small fire outdoors near the lake and burned every smoking device I owned. It was a liberating experience; though, to be frank, I missed this old "prop" for many months.

Meanwhile, I got copies of the thallium scan and consulted a couple of other experienced doctor friends. Their consensus was that since the scan can be wrong in its findings in certain areas, and since the presumed irregularities – ectopic beats, in my particular case – weren't all that extensive, I should take some other, non-invasive steps before agreeing to an angiogram. At their suggestion, I took a series of other tests, including wearing a Holter Monitor for 24 hours on a couple of occasions. None of these showed any direct relationship between the chest feeling I was still getting briefly at the outset of outdoor exercise and any presumed, measurable, cardiac difficulty. These findings were satisfactory in some ways – I felt justified in having declined the riskier test – but in others it seemed an emotional and intellectual stalemate. We still had no idea of what might be the matter. This uncertainty kept us in a troubling emotional quandary for the summer months and most of that fall. The cardiologist again called my family doctor to repeat the need for me to have an angiogram as soon as possible, but I stalled and continued my refusal.

I still believed, though doubt was growing, that I had a slight bronchial problem resulting from overexposure to the cold back in January, because there were now only certain occasions when the feeling returned. Damp, foggy mornings could be counted on to produce it. During the ragweed season it was more frequent and it seemed like an allergic reaction. I got a puffer normally used by asthma sufferers and, on the days when I remembered to use it, it seemed to provide near-instant relief. As the colder weather approached, however, the condition returned more regularly. I finally decided to go to a respirologist at a different hospital and, if possible, put an end to our wondering.

She was one of the most gentle and thorough physicians I have ever met. But all the tests she put me through for lung-related illnesses or weaknesses had completely negative results. Everything was at full capacity and working well. She then said it was time to check with the cardiology department and she recommended a particular doctor. We met soon afterwards and, although initially I had much the same reaction to him as to the first specialist, I soon became impressed by his manner and approach. I agreed to have a second stress test, this time using a cardiolite injection for the scanner to read. This type, he said, provides a more accurate picture of the amount of blood supply to the heart than the thallium scan.

I had the test on November 7 and was able to last longer and to take it at a greater speed and incline than previously. Most of the time I was jogging, almost running. I concluded the test feeling breathless, but with no other symptoms. I felt my conviction that there was no heart disease had once again been validated.

You can imagine my total disbelief, then, when some ten days later I met with the respirologist to discuss the results and I learned the truth. When I arrived in her office, she seemed very preoccupied and grave, compared with her demeanor on earlier visits. When I sat down, she said, "I have some quite disturbing news for you. The cardiologist was most alarmed when he saw the results of your scan and wants to see you as soon as possible on an emergency basis. He believes there's a serious blockage in your heart and that right now you are at great risk."

"There can't be," I said. "I walked more than seven miles this morning over a rollercoaster sideroad without any symptoms whatever."

The doctor made no specific reply. Instead, she picked up a phone, dialed a number and requested the earliest available appointment for me with the specialist. She told me, "He can see you tomorrow at 2:45 p.m."

I left her office feeling dejected and numb. It wasn't that I feared the thought of possible heart attack or death – though that was no doubt part of the package. It was the anxiety and disappointment I began to feel over what this might mean to those I love and to work that was unfinished. I dreaded having to phone Susan who I knew was anxiously awaiting my call at her downtown office. I walked up and down in the parking lot praying for some light in my confusion, for courage in my rising feeling of near-panic, and for wisdom to put this development in the gentlest possible way for Sue. I prayed quietly but aloud, to force some coherence on my efforts. It was far from simple or easy.

The following 24 hours seemed to drag on forever. I couldn't wait to meet with the cardiologist and find out exactly what he now knew about my "bronchial" affliction. When I finally sat across from him, with his large walnut desk between, I felt like I was a student again back at Oriel College, Oxford, anxiously waiting to hear what my tutor had to say to the Provost at term's end about my scholarly progress or lack thereof. I appeared outwardly calm but was inwardly quaking. The only way out of this was through it, I realized. But that was small comfort.

He told me the good news first. I had been able to get to a higher rating in the test (stage 5) than most men my age because of all my walking and "remarkable general fitness." The monitors had shown some ectopic beats during the exercise but nothing very extraordinary.

"However, when we come to the cardiolite scan itself – the point where we get to see the actual blood supply to your heart during exercise," he continued, "the evidence is unmistakably clear. Under such stress, there is a totally inadequate profusion of blood in one of the most crucial areas of your heart. Obviously there's a large blockage in the LAD artery. My guess is that probably 95 percent of that artery has been obstructed by plaque. You are currently, therefore, at extreme risk of a massive, and so quite possibly fatal, heart attack. You must have an angiogram as soon as it can be arranged, definitely before Christmas. Meanwhile, no more long walks, climbing hills, or any other kind of exertion. Take the daily aspirin and also a beta-blocker. Be sure to carry your nitro spray at all times."

If I had been shocked before, this time I felt devastated. I accepted his prescriptions for a renewed supply of the medicines and walked out of there almost like an automaton. What and how was I going to tell Susan now? I walked again in the parking lot for a long while and prayed more fervently than I had ever done, before calling her. I felt let down, betrayed somehow by God, and so, increasingly angry. The why? of earlier prayer now had a bitter edge. What was the good of prayer and of trust, I raged, if this was the way they were received and answered?

Somehow, though, as I gradually prayed and thought about it all more clearly, I began to realize that in spite of the bad news there was now a sort of clarity to the situation that had evaded us before. The "enemy" had been named, the problem seemingly unmasked, a course of action had been set in motion, and finally an end to our uncertainty was in sight. To my surprise, when I eventually called and told Susan, her reaction after the initial shock was one of at least partial relief as well. We had a lot to discuss that evening.

The doctor's secretary phoned the next day with an appointment for the angiogram at The Toronto Hospital in about two weeks. This itself was a clear indication of the urgency of the situation because all the medical specialists in the province of Ontario were observing a work slowdown and bookings for a "normal" angiogram were being delayed by three months or more. I was by now looking forward to getting it over with but a lot had to be done in a hurry – chest X-rays taken, an electrocardiogram done and several other medical tests as well. I wrote several of my Sunday *Star* columns ahead in case I wouldn't feel like writing after the surgery.

For those happily unfamiliar with angiography I should briefly explain that it involves making a small but deep incision into an artery in the groin – in the fold area where the thigh joins the torso – and introducing a long catheter with a tiny camera at the tip. This is manipulated painlessly so as to finally reach the heart itself. The process can actually be watched by the patient on a television monitor. At one point, a dye is infused into the heart, producing a warm rush from one's toes to the crown of the head. More photos are taken. A complete and totally accurate picture of the heart from all angles is thus achieved. On this basis decisions can then be made on whether a bypass, angioplasty, or whatever, is necessary.

The findings of the angiogram were dramatic and, to me at any rate, most surprising. About halfway into the examination, the cardiologist in charge pointed to the screen and showed me where the LAD artery was indeed not only *mostly* blocked but *completely* so. "You've got a 100 percent blockage there," he said. When I quickly commented that I must have some very good collateral arteries to make up for this huge loss of circulation – because of the very limited discomfort produced by the second stress test and exercise in general – he said, "Somebody's been doing some reading I see." He went on to say he'd talk about the situation further as soon as the angiogram was over, and I was wheeled to recovery.

When he did come to chat, his news, though seemingly ambiguous at first, brought a hugely welcome relief. The bad news was the total blockage of such a crucial artery. The good news was that the collateral system of tiny arteries, devised by the body in response to the deepening crisis in the LAD artery and because of my exercise regime, was truly quite extensive. Unless stressed unduly, it was all that would be required. My heart, it seems, had produced its own means of bypassing the blockage. The doctor said that no further invasive tests or remedies were anticipated. All that would be necessary would be a small dose of daily aspirin and a very mild beta-blocker. I felt enormously relieved and could scarcely wait to see Susan who was waiting in the hospital room. When she heard the story she shared fully in my sense of thankfulness for prayer that had been so strangely answered. Mysterious and at first ominous though it appeared, in personal terms it was one of life's "miracles."

When I returned in a few days to the office of my own cardiologist for his assessment of the results, the elevator took forever to come and so I decided to walk up the four long flights to his office rather than wait. When I told him what I had just done, he laughed and said, "There can't be much wrong with you, then, that's for sure." He went on to confirm that, because of the gradual collateral development over the years, there was not, as he had originally speculated, a great risk of heart attack, certainly as far as the blocked artery was concerned. The remaining good news was that the other main arteries were wide open or "patent." There was absolutely no need for a bypass or other surgery. I went from fearing I might be under close medical supervision for the rest of my life to hearing him say he would see me in about one year for a further checkup.

At this point, I am pleased to report that I quickly resumed my morning walks and that in spite of even cold weather I now rarely experience the former mild angina at all.

Susan and I are now committed to following closely Dr. Dean Ornish's stricter program, the one aimed at reversal. We believe, rightly or wrongly, that the blockage can be reduced and that any further build-up of plaque in the other two arteries can also be avoided.[4]

The program, while it seems at first to be one of self-denial and hardship, has given us a great improvement in overall quality of life beyond anything we dreamed of. I enjoy not just the low-fat, vegetarian diet and exercise program, I know we both are really profiting spiritually from the discipline of regular yoga and meditation – the practice of paying much more attention to the "now," to *being* instead of doing, and to the mind-body relationship in general.

The truth is that the discovery that I have some heart disease is proving to have been an important wake-up call in my life. Though I never thought I would say this, my ongoing prayers for health or wholeness have been answered in God's own and better way. I am frankly grateful it happened to me as it did. I owe so much to it already, and so does my wife.

UPDATE

In late November 1997, almost exactly one year from the final diagnosis of my coronary artery disease, I went back to the same hospital for a repeat of the full cardiolite stress test, as the cardiologist had requested 12 months previously. When we met a few days later for his assessment and summing up of the results, the news was all good. The latest blood work had shown a remarkable drop in cholesterol on the low- to no-fat diet and my average blood pressure had dropped close to 20 points on either side of the equation – diastolic and systolic. Most encouraging, I was able to go a full ten minutes on the tilted treadmill before I stopped. (The complete run can go 13 minutes.)

True, there was still a major blockage in the LAD artery but the charts revealed that the overall blood flow, while similar to the last time, seemed slightly better than before. Since coronary artery disease usually gets worse year by year, coupled with the fact that my energy levels had been much higher for the past months and that I had been almost completely free from chest discomfort during daily walks even when climbing hills, he felt satisfied that progress was being made. It was possible, he said, that a slight reversal had occurred but that the cardiolite scan wasn't precise enough to show this for certain. His final words to me were, "Go on living your life to the fullest doing whatever it is you're doing to try to improve your health. Come and see me again in a year."

––––––––––

Significantly, the doctor told me he had just taken part in a nationwide poll of physicians conducted by *Maclean's*, Canada's most prestigious weekly news magazine. The reporter told him,

to the doctor's surprise although he is a very devout Orthodox
Jew, that the majority of the nation's doctors also say they believe in prayer and that it plays an important role in their healing
work. Later, I saw the story in *Maclean's* for myself. More and
more Canadian doctors are using spiritual healing, the magazine
said. Increasingly they are recommending meditation, yoga, and
prayer to help patients reduce stress. It reported that all but a few
Canadian doctors believe in God and 69 percent pray at least
from time to time. Not that they get down on their knees with
their patients or anything like that; it's simply that they realize
their own limitations and the great mysteries of the human condition. Many simply said they felt a great need to call upon the
power and wisdom of the "Great Healer" day by day.[5]

A PRACTICAL APPLICATION

Reflect upon your own life and discover whether you have had
any similar experiences. List them in order of importance and
then write them out in at least brief notes. You will then find it
easy as well as spiritually helpful to give thanks for all those
"unanswered prayers" that, in the end, turned out to have been
answers as good as, or even much better than, those you originally sought and pleaded for.

III

PRAYING
"THE LORD'S PRAYER"

I don't know who – or what – put the question, I don't know when it was put. I don't even remember answering. But at some moment I did answer Yes to Someone – or Something – and that from that hour I was certain that existence is meaningful and that, therefore, my life in self-surrender, had a goal. From that moment I have known what it means "not to look back," and "to take no thought for the morrow."

Dag Hammarskjöld, *Markings*,

translated by Leif Sjoberg and W. H. Auden, 1964

———

My father! The Great Spirit is my father!
The earth is my mother – and on her bosom I will recline...
Tecumseh (1768-1813), Chief of the Shawnees,

at the Council at Vincennes, Indiana Territory, Aug. 14, 1810

At the outset, I commented about the way in which the subject of prayer is coming to the fore today in the media and in many new books. Two of these books, to which I have referred several times in my newspaper columns, seem important to me. It's significant that they're both by eminent doctors who have specialized in research. One is *Prayer is Good Medicine* by Larry Dossey, former co-chair of the Panel on Mind/Body Interventions for the American National Institute of Health. The other, cited already, is *Timeless Healing, The Power and Biology of Belief*, by Herbert Benson, a leading professor at Harvard Medical School's Mind-Body Institute. Sceptics who scoff that prayer is "the mind's soliloquy to itself" will find that these books and others like them challenge the sceptic's own dogmas with the kind of evidence they claim to respect most – hard data, empirical results. More research such as these works present will continue to be published in the near future as old models of science and the universe increasingly give way to new, more comprehensive paradigms.

That kind of research work and a scientific approach to our subject are of tremendous importance. My present aim, however, is humbler but hopefully more practical, more basic. Here I want to share some personal thoughts about one of the archetypal prayers of all time, commonly called "The Lord's Prayer." My thinking on this was push-started recently when a column reader called to get advice on a discussion he was having. His friend, a Jew, was arguing that this prayer is really a Jewish prayer and not just the property of Christians and the church.

There's a lot to be said for that view. Jesus was and remained a pious Jew all his life. There's not a single word in the prayer that a strict Jew of his day could not have uttered in complete fidelity to the God of Moses, of Israel and of the cosmos. It truly is a fully Jewish prayer in every way. But it's also more. As a matter of interest, the near-total universality of the prayer is obvious once you make a study of the prayers of other faiths, including, as we will see below, those belonging to aboriginal peoples around the globe. Historically, however, it has been so identified with Christianity that it has become widely known and accepted as the quintessential Christian prayer. Consequently, as is so often the truth in religious differences once you get past externals, both sides in my caller's debate were right in their own way!

Scholars believe the title, The Lord's Prayer, is somewhat misleading and that a more accurate one would be, The Disciples' Prayer. This is not just a question of semantics or of typically academic nit-picking. According to the account of the prayer given in Luke 11:1 and following, it's the prayer Jesus taught his disciples in response to their specific request, "Lord, teach us to pray." Incidentally, each gospel writer has his own spiritual or theological interests. Luke says more about prayer, for example, and about women's roles than do the others. In Luke's version, the disciples had just seen Jesus himself at prayer and so asked for guidance as "John [the Baptist] taught his disciples." On the other hand, Matthew omits this context and, somewhat artificially, puts the prayer right in the middle of the Sermon on the Mount. He introduces it with some general observations on the wrong way and the wrong reasons for praying: for example, using meaningless repetitions or praying in public in order to be seen by others (Matthew 6:5ff). Of course, it's possible Jesus used it himself and that it was thus also his prayer, but there's no specific record that he actually ever did so. The longest prayer in the New Testament, ascribed to Jesus, is the one which constitutes the entire 17th chapter of John's gospel. It has importance for another aspect of this account later on in the book.

That said, while recently rereading Simone Weil's powerful little book *Waiting for God*, I rediscovered that she emphatically confirms what I (with millions of others down the ages) have found – that regularly praying this prayer, with deep concentration and focus, is one of the most satisfying spiritual experiences one can have.[1] If you work with it, if you look for its deep bite on your life and the lives of others, it never ceases to comfort, to fortify, and to challenge – all at the same time.

"OUR FATHER WHO ART IN HEAVEN..."

By the words, "Our Father who art in heaven," (Luke leaves out the words following Father) we put ourselves into the presence of the One who is both an intimate father-mother-friend and the utterly transcendent Source of all being. The words "our father" signify God's immanent, loving closeness to each one of us. In his Letter to the Romans, Paul makes it very clear that for the earliest disciples the characteristic first experience upon conversion was the ability, as well as the need, through the Spirit's inner promptings, to call God by the most intimate of names – "Abba" (Romans 8:15). If you change the two b's to p's (a frequent occurrence in moving from Greek to English) and add a "p" at the beginning, you have our word "pappa." Abba itself, however, comes from the language spoken by Jesus and the first Christians – Aramaic. In the original version of the prayer, it was undoubtedly the word used by Jesus. It denotes deep, affectionate intimacy and probably can be best translated by our English word, "Daddy." In the relevant passage, Paul writes, "...you have received a spirit of adoption. When we cry: 'Abba! Father!' it is that very Spirit bearing witness with our spirit that we are children of God..."

The imagery of God as our "Father" is probably the clearest evidence of the prayer's universality. It is by no means original on the part of Jesus. *The Oxford Book of Prayer* gives several examples from other faiths, some much earlier than Christianity.[2] Here, for instance, is a Shinto prayer from Japan: "I reverently speak in the presence of the Great Parent God..." One ancient Jewish prayer still used today begins: "Cause us, our Father, to lie down in peace and rise again to enjoy life..." A key Hindu prayer says: "O God, you are our Providence and our Father...You are called Father, caring for the humble." A Sioux Indian prayer similarly commences: "Ho! Great Spirit, Grandfather, you have made everything and are in everything..." The Greeks and Romans regularly wrote and spoke of Zeus as "Father of the gods and of men."

But there's a real problem with suggesting automatically that everyone should address God or the Source of all Being as "father." Today, with our increased sensitivity over sexism and patriarchy on all fronts, but particularly in religion and spirituality, coupled with the fact of widespread parental or institutional abuse of children – mostly by males and, most tragic of all, too often in religious settings of one kind or another – the very idea of calling God "Father" can be extremely repugnant. For many people searching for a deeper experience of spiritual things, such male terminology sends all the wrong messages. If the earliest memories of one's own father were or still are terrifying, or associated with sexual abuse, or even with a harsh, arbitrary severity, a drinking problem, or whatever, projecting this "into the heavens" so to speak can warp one's thoughts and feelings about the ultimate object of prayer forever. The same is true if the abuser was someone widely called "Father" by the religious community itself.

This enormous difficulty has not yet, I believe, been sufficiently addressed by any major religious body, with the exception
of some forms of Hinduism, and the Baha'is. True, it can be of
some help when new liturgies in some churches change the word-
ing of the "Our Father" to read, "Our Father/Mother" or "Our
Supreme Parent," but this only helps a certain group of people
within the shrinking number who still go to church. And ultra-
conservative elements in all denominations, particularly in the
Roman Catholic Church, the largest branch of all, continue to
fight against such changes. For many more, the entire idea of any
parent-type imagery to speak of God has negative vibrations or
implications. For that reason, it's highly important to keep re-
minding ourselves that all the words used to describe the vast
mystery we know as God are essentially analogical or metaphorical. If your major problem with truly praying is rooted in the fact
that the traditional terms do not help you, get rid of them or you
will never find prayer meaningful at all. In truth, there are times
when even those who feel quite comfortable with the father or
mother words need to shake their prayer life up by employing a
whole set of other descriptions or imagery – for example, "Friend,"
or "Great Spirit," or "Creator," or "Lord of the Universe." Most
certainly there is a word-picture or metaphor out there which
you can find uniquely suited to your needs and your inmost sense
of self and of Ultimate Reality. "Divine Light" or "Lord of Divine
Light" is a form of address that on many occasions rises to my
own mind and heart when I begin to pray.

This whole matter is one that I have had to struggle long
and hard with in my own journey. Let me be quite personal for
a moment. My father died suddenly in 1968 at the age of only
62 and I still miss him very much today. I have, like many sons,
come to understand and appreciate my father so much more

since his death than I ever did before. He was an outstanding person in so many ways, with an amazing energy level and a keen desire to do whatever he did to the best of his abilities. He was liked and admired by a very diverse group of people. Certainly he had very high ambitions and expectations for all of us, especially for me, his firstborn.Yet, while charming with people at work and elsewhere outside the home, he was an extremely forceful, authoritative, even chauvinistic tyrant in many ways towards his four children, two boys and two girls. He had a very low tolerance for weakness of any kind on our part and, to be fair, also regarding himself. I once made the mistake – at about age 14 – of telling him I had a headache. He told me to snap out of it. "I've never had a headache in my whole life," he said.

He could on occasion be quite arbitrary and unreasonable in any father-child conflicts. One day in my teens I arrived home to see my beloved dog, Pat, being led into the back of a Humane Society wagon. I was astounded and asked what was going on. My mother told me, "Your father has decided it's time we got rid of him," and that was it. No amount of pleading or grieving on our part would have availed to change his mind. I recall a time when he became annoyed by my younger brother's penchant for mechanical and electrical experimentation. George, at about 12 years old, had rigged up a crystal radio set and some form of phone line between our house and the house of his chum across the street.The two boys would lie awake for hours at night either talking to one another or listening to a favorite radio program. My father suddenly swooped into George's room, took the radio and earphones, and later buried them in the fresh concrete of a walkway he was repairing in the backyard. One could go on. He had lot of anger and he didn't believe in suppressing it.

At the same time he was profoundly religious and submitted us in our earliest years to a kind of fundamentalism which taught a narrow vision of a very angry God who had laid down one way only for human salvation. It was an interpretation of the gospels which exalted the idea of Christ's "bloody sacrifice" for sin, and of an apocalyptic end to all things. The little Gospel Hall he forced us to attend in our earliest years featured many sermons on the topic of Armageddon. I know that those itinerant lay preachers literally scared the hell out of me and led to my going up to the front of the church and "being saved" on several Sunday evenings before I was 14. I remember walking home with him one night after one of these end-of-the-world specials and confiding in my dad, with tears in my eyes, that I didn't think I'd ever make it into heaven. His reply? "You worry too much. Forget about it." But, in truth, the overwhelming impact of all the emphasis on sin, hell, and lakes of fire at the Gospel Hall was leading to a miserably low sense of self-esteem for myself and to a very negative view of human nature in general. This response stayed with me for a long time.

He loved being the leader, especially if it involved a uniform of some sort. I never knew a time when he was not at the front of the room as I grew up, superintending the Sunday school, leading a boys' band – trumpet, flute, you name it – or calling out marching orders to his company of the Boys' Brigade, of which, of course, I was a member. That, along with the combination of my own sensitivity, his rather belligerent temperament, and his stern religion during my boyhood, made a lasting, almost indelible stamp on my mind. It was easy to project our already warped, childish notions of God onto him since he adopted a very godlike posture in our lives.

Indeed, he continued to call most of the shots in my life until I was almost 30, including what church I would attend during my three years as an undergraduate at Oxford, what theological college I would go to for ministerial training afterwards, and even where I would teach theology eventually. It took me many years to have the courage to rebel against both his theology and his desire to live a considerable part of his life through me. Thankfully, as he began to study theology himself – eventually taking a diploma and being ordained as an Anglican priest – he became much more liberal and open to dialogue. But, in any case, for many years now I have found that I can finally call God "Father" without feeling echoes of the more negative side of my own father experience. I'm grateful to have been able to separate the metaphor from its earliest psychological resonances. But all of that struggle has given me a great sympathy for those who continue to be caught in the same kind of confusion. If the father image puts you off, avoid it completely, at least for now.

The words, "Who art in heaven" have caused much confusion over the ages. It does not mean that God is off in some distant, galactic space or place but that the One who is "closer than our own breathing" simultaneously transcends the whole of reality. This God is everywhere, within us and without. God is the very ground of our being. In his well-known speech to a crowd of sceptical Greeks on Mars Hill, the Areopagus in Athens, recorded in Acts 17, Paul cites as evidence for this omnipresent, transcendent reality, the so-called pagan authors with whom the members of his audience were most familiar. He first reminds them that God is not only the source of all things, but the One who has "made of one blood all nations." He then goes on to say that we are always in the divine presence: "...indeed God is not far from each one of us. For in God we live and move and have our being; as even some of your own poets have said, 'For we too are God's offspring'" (*An Inclusive-Language Lectionary*).

"HALLOWED BE THY NAME.
THY KINGDOM COME,
THY WILL BE DONE ON EARTH..."

The first three petitions in the prayer are poorly understood even by those who recite them most often. They have become so automatic and dulled by overfamiliarity and dry repetition that they unfortunately tend to run off us like the proverbial water off a duck. Anyone who knows the very ancient Jewish prayer, the Kaddish (still in use today), will observe the very Jewish nature at the core of the petitions. The Kaddish begins like this: "May his great name be magnified and sanctified in the world which he has created according to his will. May he cause his kingdom to rule and his redemption to shoot forth, and may he bring near his Messiah and redeem his people in your life and in your days, and in the life of the house of Israel...speedily, and at a near time."[3]

"Hallowed be thy name" means, "may your name (your full character and nature) be sanctified, or honored and kept sacred." In all religious writings, indeed in all ancient fairy tales (for example, Rumpelstiltskin) and old mythologies as well, the name of various characters, including gods, is always pregnant with meaning and highly reverenced. Names and name changes were very potent realities. For example, consider the change of Jacob's name to Israel; or Cephas' name to Peter (from the Greek word, *petros*, a rock), the apostle whose faith was like a rock. In his 1981 commentary called *The Gospel According to Matthew*, the late F. W. Beare noted the following: "The Old Testament prophets charge that God's own people profane his name when they are unfaithful and disobedient, when they engage in the sexual profligacies of the Canaanite shrines...or when the rich cheat the poor and the strong oppress the weak."[4]

One way to personalize this petition and to make it come alive is to expand it a little. For example, we could say, "Hallowed be thy name – in my own thoughts, life, and work today; in our home, in our neighborhood, in our nation; in the way we treat others, especially the poor or outcasts of society; in the way we relate to the Earth; in the example I and those whom I love set for others"; even in the way we drive, and so forth. A moment's meditation on some of the real ramifications of what we are truly asking for here can lead to a transformation of our praying and of our living too.

One can do the same with "Thy kingdom come, Thy will be done on Earth..." by going on to add specific instances in our own lives or elsewhere that particularly need to feel and know the presence and rule of the living God. For example, "May your kingdom come and your will be done in our common life as we Canadians (Americans, British, or whoever) seek a more just and healing society." Or, "May your sovereignty be acknowledged and your will be done in my personal life in this or that area where I am currently being defeated, tempted, or made aware that I am off course from my higher self." This passage can be extremely helpful when our goals have become confused or our overall sense of focus has departed leaving us treading water or perhaps at risk of "drowning." We long to see clearly once again, to be able to move ahead.

"GIVE US THIS DAY OUR DAILY BREAD; AND FORGIVE US OUR DEBTS, AS WE FORGIVE OUR DEBTORS; AND LEAD US NOT INTO TEMPTATION, BUT DELIVER US FROM EVIL..."

The next four petitions of "the Lord's Prayer" focus more sharply still upon God's relevance and action in our immediate concerns of day-to-day living. But, once again, scholars are still quick to point out their extremely Jewish character. As Frank Beare wrote in his commentary on Matthew, "There is not a single clause that is without parallels in Jewish prayers known to us" (p. 175).

The prayer for daily bread, of course, includes not just our physical needs and those of all other creatures on the planet, but the soul-nurturing we all need in order to keep and foster our true humanity. Incidentally, the very familiar translation of the Greek original as "our daily bread" is probably incorrect. The word rendered by "daily" never means that elsewhere in Greek. The correct translation is most likely, "Give us today *sufficient* bread for the day."

As we go on to ask for forgiveness – "And forgive us our debts [trespasses] as we forgive our debtors [those who trespass against us]" – we are reminded always of the deep connection between our own readiness to forgive others and our experience of true forgiveness for ourselves. Oftentimes we expect peace of mind and divine forgiveness while we are actually carrying a large load of resentment and of failure to forgive wrongs real or imagined committed by others against us. There's a strong sense in the prayer that God's forgiveness is deeply attached to the condition that we first forgive those who are somehow indebted to us or who have offended us. Again this belongs to general Jewish spirituality. For example, Ben Sirach says, "Forgive your neighbor the wrong he has done, and then your sins will be pardoned when you pray."

My personal experience, however, makes me take the petition and the apparent condition to a deeper, psychological level as well. I have found that it is very difficult indeed to fully accept the truth that one is forgiven by the Author and Ground of the cosmos if there remains a backlog in mind and heart of resentment and hostility towards any group or individual who has really or seemingly injured or offended us. On the contrary, when you take the initiative and forgive those who you may have totally solid arguments for believing are deeply in the wrong, the inner way for receiving forgiveness yourself is opened very wide. There is a flow of inner joy that the spoiled relationship with neighbors, relatives or genuine enemies has been rectified or at least had the sting removed. At the same time, the relief of feeling and knowing oneself to be now truly forgiven by God is enormous. It's as though some inner blockage has been removed and the "water of life" is suddenly bubbling up within us once more.

Part of the final petition is missing in the original account given by Luke. According to the earliest manuscripts, he says only: "And do not bring us to the time of trial." The reference is thought by many interpreters (exegetes) to be to the time of fiery testing believed to be coming as a precursor to the end of all things. Certainly the first Christians, Paul in particular – though, from my own research, probably not Jesus himself – appear to have shared the conviction that the end of the world was in sight. But, for moderns, whether Christian or not, the full meaning is not concerned with some kind of end-time angst but with the temptations and trials of daily living.

Matthew says, "Lead us not into temptation (a time of trial or testing) but deliver us from evil." Some later manuscripts read, "But deliver us from the Evil One." Here again scholars believe the earlier versions are correct. Furthermore, this request to God only becomes a genuine heart-cry for help when we go on to think specifically of our own problems or those of others and name them.

There are not only the specific evils of disease, or other potential calamities to include here. We need to include in this petition divine protection from the harm or hatred – perhaps even unknown to us – being directed towards us by those who are enemies. You can try to love your enemies and to forgive them, but not to surround oneself with "the armor of God," as Paul calls it, is overly naive and an opening of oneself to real harm. As Dr. Larry Dossey argues in his book *Prayer is Good Medicine*, if prayer works in a positive fashion, the same "energy" from malicious sources conceivably can affect us negatively if we refuse to take adequate care.

By this kind of deeper approach, I have found that these otherwise clichéd and rather obscure requests alone can become a source of real guidance and power in facing the decisions of one's life. Otherwise the whole prayer is just a quaint form of pious repetition.

"FOR THINE IS THE KINGDOM, THE POWER AND THE GLORY..."

The final words, "For thine is the kingdom, the power and the glory..." may well not have been part of the original prayer. Contrary to popular belief, they do not appear in either Matthew or Luke, the two places in the gospels devoted to "the Lord's Prayer." When I say this I'm referring to the earliest gospel manuscripts, those written before the fifth century CE. They certainly *do* appear in those thousands of copies of the New Testament which came later, but this is obviously a case of subsequent addition by overly zealous scribes. The "doxology," as these words are called, does occur, however, in one early Christian document which was widely used to train catechumens or beginners. It's called the *Didache* or Teaching, and can be dated roughly to the middle of the second century.

Nevertheless, late or not, the passage is certainly inspired by the Spirit and affords a chance for lifting up one's whole inner life in thanksgiving and praise of the Creator. It's a move from *asking* to *affirmation* and an appropriate point at which to be specific again – this time listing things for which one is most thankful.

FOR FURTHER REFLECTION
AND ACTION

For anyone wanting to learn more about what the earliest tradition, especially the author(s)/editors of Matthew's gospel thought about "The Lord's Prayer" and its extended meaning, the best thing to do is to read the balance of the Sermon on the Mount in Matthew 6:14 to 7:28. Bible scholars have frequently offered the opinion that this latter part of the Sermon on the Mount is really a development of the prayer itself and I agree.

In any case, if you feel a deep need to grow in prayer now and in the years ahead (and who that is consciously on the spiritual path doesn't?), this prayer can be the best place for you to make a fresh start. It can be prayed daily – on the subway, in your car while commuting or on a casual drive, at the office or any other kind of work station, even while walking down the street or through the woods – by those of all faiths and of none. All that is required is to pray each petition with quiet concentration as though it were for the very first time.

One final thought. Not long ago, just after we had prayed it aloud together, Susan pointed out something to me about this prayer that I had never really noticed before. She said, "You know, it's a very demanding kind of prayer. I mean, the tone is not so much one of politely asking as of virtually telling God what's required. It has all the bluntness of a three-year-old child making legitimate claims on his or her parents."

As I have reflected on this since, I can't think of ever hearing or reading that kind of commentary on the prayer before. But it's true. Apart from the phrase requesting that God's will be done in all things, the petitions are fairly peremptory. They're made with confidence, even with some *élan*. Clearly Jesus didn't think the proper approach to his "Father" was one of overly pious servility or of fawning, highly conditional, "if you please" abasement. Jesus' attitude to prayer is that one can dare to be bold. If God is truly supreme and yet our intimate Friend and "Shepherd," if we truly are God's children, we have every right to expect our prayers to be answered and to lay out our requests with openness and courage. As Jesus himself reminded his followers, "Ask and you shall have; seek and you shall find; knock and it shall be opened unto you" (Matthew 7:7–8).

PART TWO

GOING
WITHIN

But whenever you pray,
go into your room and shut the door
and pray to God who is in secret;
and God who sees in secret
will reward you.

Matthew 6:6

(*An Inclusive-Language Lectionary*)

IV

THE GOD WITHIN

Religion (or more properly spirituality) is, in fact,
a severely practical and empirical kind of research.
You take nothing on trust.
You accept nothing but your own experience.
You go forward step by step, like an explorer in a virgin jungle,
to see what you will find.

The Yoga Aphorisms of Patanjali

(Hollywood, CA: Vedanta Press, 1953), p. 86

Be still and know that I am God.

Psalm 46:10

The Kingdom of God is within you.

Jesus, Luke 17:21

————————

It is the God within your own self that is impelling you to seek him,
to realize him. After long searches here and there,
in temples and in churches, on earth and in heaven,
at last you come back to your own soul...
and find that he whom you have been seeking all over the world,
for whom you have been weeping and praying...
is the nearest of the near...

Swami Vivekananda (1896) Jnana Yoga.

New York; Ramakrishna-Vivekananda Center, 1955

The Creator, the Source of all Being, the Ultimate Mystery we call God, is the One to whom and with whom we pray. This is the case no matter by what names this Divinity is known or through whatever intermediaries her presence is or has been sought. For example, despite what Christianity has traditionally taught about Hinduism, behind the seemingly bewildering number of deities called upon in different situations and traditions by Hindus, there is the never-changing, omnipresent, omnipotent Brahman, "first-born and foremost among the Gods. From him sprang the universe..." (The Upanishads). When you cut through the outer trappings, the Great Spirit, or divine "Grandfather" to whom prayer is made in North American Indian spirituality, is discernibly the same reality to whom Christians pray in the name (that is, according to the revelation given in him) of Jesus, or whom Jews follow according to the Torah which is believed to have been first revealed to Moses. Indeed, it has been my experience – both from my reading and from my journalistic travels for several decades now – that the more I study all the major world religions and look beneath their surfaces, the more I'm convinced that they are amazingly similar in their essential beliefs and aims. I found this particularly to be the case when researching the topics of life after death and of spiritual healing. The same has been true in examining the attitudes and approaches to prayer of the various religions.

But as one struggles for a better understanding and practice of prayer, one is brought face-to-face with another issue as well, one involving a different sort of question: *Where* is the God whom we seek to address or with whom we feel such an urgent need to converse? In what direction, so to speak, are we to aim our praying? We saw in our look at "the Lord's Prayer" that to say "who art in heaven" does not mean that the God to whom we pray is in some intergalactic heavenly place, sitting on a throne and surrounded by all the appurtenances of an ancient royal court. That kind of literalism is based mainly, in my view, upon a failure to understand the metaphorical or analogical nature of all speech about God and related matters.

True, millions of believers in the past have placed God "out there," and many still think in those literalistic, spatial terms today. I know, for I have myself often borne their wrath on scores of talk shows in the U.S. and Canada, or in letters of outrage to the editors of newspapers across the country. Old sillinesses often die hard. By "in heaven" we are speaking metaphorically of God's transcendence, his/her "beyondness" or "otherness." It's not about a spatial place of dwelling but about a mode or dimension of being. Like most people, it took me a long time before I was able to make the switch from childhood beliefs that God actually abides in the kind of place a space rocket should eventually be able to penetrate – if only it could be fueled sufficiently to get really "out there" – to the awareness that God fills all space, is contained nowhere, yet present everywhere.

With the exception of the strictest forms of Buddhism (for example, Theraveda Buddhism, now dominant in Sri Lanka and Southeast Asia), when you look deeply at the major world religions, you find two truths held simultaneously.

The first is that God does not so much "exist" as she is existence itself. In God, to repeat Paul's famous line once more, we live and move and have our very being; for, he is not far from any one of us.

At the same time, this God, this Spiritual Essence, dwells within us, every one of us no matter how much we ignore, deny or offend against this Reality; no matter how we feel; no matter how far we stray from the divine will for our lives. God is an inner reality – once again called by many different names. In Taoism, there is the *Te*, or part of the *Tao*, the overarching Way, the final reality embracing all things and directing the "flow" of life. This *Te* is within each one of us. In Hinduism, you have the *Atman* within, the divine Higher Self which is part of the universal Atman or Brahman. True awakening comes when you one day realize that God is within you, that in a profound sense you too are divine. "You are That," as the Hindu rishis and gurus for centuries have put it. In Christianity and Judaism, there is the *Imago Dei*, the image of God according to which we humans have been created. Genesis says that our very breath, the subtle link between our spirit, mind, and body, was breathed into our mythical ancestor, Adam, by the Creator. The text is explicit. God breathed into his nostrils the breath of life, "And the man became a living soul" (KJV). More, much more, is being said in this famous passage than that God gives us the gift of life. The various animals are given that as well. The image of God refers to the gift of self-reflective consciousness, of moral freedom and of spiritual and creative capacities virtually unlimited. We are the offspring of God and thus the actual bearers of Divine Breath or Spirit.

But that is not all. The psalmist talks about God's Spirit dwelling within us. For example, he prays, "Take not thy holy Spirit from us." The opening lines of John's gospel put the Christ Event in a cosmic setting. The author, instead of giving us another version of the birth narratives of Matthew and Luke, makes it clear that the Logos or Word of God – "the True Light" – actually "gives light" to every person who comes into the world (who is born into the human family). The "light that lighteth every person who comes into the world" is always within us (John 1:9, my translation). It's what we do with it that counts.

Jesus' own teaching in the first three gospels, the synoptics, about the Kingdom or reign of God and the fact that it is "within" us, as well as outside us, is a variation on this same theme. Thus, as Matthew describes it, he was able to say to his followers: *"You are the light of the world"* (Matthew 5:14). As George Fox, a Quaker, used to say: "There is that of God within us." Of course, he also used the symbolism of "the light within" constantly. The "inner light" is the virtual motto and creed of Quakers (The Society of Friends) today. The sacred scriptures of Sikhism say, "God is concealed in every heart; his light is in every heart." Other examples from other faiths abound.

It would take an entire book to discuss fully the Apostle Paul's "take" on this same truth. The Spirit of God within us – even praying within us – is one way he works out his mysticism, his belief in our identification and intimacy with the divine Presence within. To confirm this for yourself, read (or reread) his Letter to the Romans, chapter 8. In one well-known passage, 1 Corinthians 3:16, he writes, "Do you not know that you are God's temple and that God's Spirit dwells in you?" In addition, there is his whole teaching about the Christian believer being "in Christ," or the reverse of this, his many references to "Christ in you."

In passing, it seems to elude fundamentalists, who believe there has been one unchanging version of "the gospel" since the teaching of Jesus himself, that Paul makes some very key changes to the original teaching. This is also a big topic, too complex for full treatment here; but, let me give one crucial example, highly relevant to our discussion.

Christians and non-Christians alike can test this for themselves. Jesus, in the gospels, constantly spoke of God's reign, God's Kingdom. He did so in three ways. It was the Kingdom which was in one sense already here, which nevertheless was also in the process of coming immediately in a fresh way in his ministry, and which would one day come in even greater power and fulfillment. That was the essence of his gospel or good news, the Reign of God. Jesus proclaimed that, in spite of appearances to the contrary, God is in ultimate control. But Paul, whose writings compose about a third of the New Testament, only uses the concept – and the actual words from the gospels, "the Kingdom of God" or "the Kingdom of Heaven" (which means the same thing but piously avoids using the name, God) – once or twice at most.

This is a striking phenomenon when you examine it. Paul has changed the characteristic language of Jesus about the Kingdom to his own phrase, *en Christo*, in Christ. This latter expression occurs in his writings constantly. But, you see, he was interested in communicating with the Greek-speaking world of his day. In Greek, the phrase *He Basileia tou Theou*, the Kingdom of God, was bewildering and awkward. And the idea expressed by it, though rich in its Hebrew background and meaning, meant virtually nothing to most gentiles. On the other hand, in a culture which at that time was full of myths and stories of mystical identification with descending, dying, and reascending gods (for example, in the Mystery Religions), to speak of being "in" a redeemer or of having this representative of a god "in you" was to be instantly understood. Sacred meals, baptism in water, or even the blood of some ritual sacrifice such as a bull (the initiates stood under a metal grating on which the bull was slaughtered) were all rituals conveying a part of this sense of union.

To return to our main theme, most people tend to believe that Eastern and Western spirituality differ widely. The West has put God "out there," and so has made prayer a kind of projection of thoughts and requests "outwards" to an external Being; the East has seemingly internalized and made God the God within. It's important, however, to realize that the alleged difference is only in appearance. True, both have their own major "tilt" or tradition when it comes to this issue. But, in actuality, each retains both emphases. What's more, both are crucial, in my experience and judgment, for a full and balanced understanding of our relationship with the Divine.

There are times when we are overcome by our sense of God's transcendence, by our awe and gratitude at the beauty and the wonder of the natural world, at the magnificence of a piece of art or some particular piece of music – or by our awareness of some aspect of global suffering and global danger. At these times, we reach out in our prayers to God's presence throughout the whole of the cosmos. We pray to God around us and over us and in all things. But there are other times, and increasingly I find these are in the majority, when we feel the urge and need to look within, to God manifest in our own Higher Self. A great surge of interest in meditation and in how to commune with the Divine within us is revealing itself widely in Western society today. The reason is that the old ideas of a great superparent in the sky, erroneously inculcated by mainstream Christianity and some other faiths in the past – and sharply criticized by nonbelievers such as Sigmund Freud – are no longer tenable for the great majority. These ideas offend the intellect and, in practice, are the source of much of the enormous disillusionment with formal prayer and with traditional religious institutions that is still growing in Western society, in spite of the renewed interest in prayer itself. Few things cater more to a lapse of zest and of authenticity in praying than persisting in prayers, particularly those of a rigid or liturgical kind, which are directed solely to a remote, austere God-of-the-Vast-Void, "out there somewhere" far away.

The kind of experience that people who are keenly aware they are on a spiritual journey want and need today is an intimacy with the God who is immanent in all creation, and particularly in the human heart or soul or Higher Self. There is again a plethora of ways to describe this truth. But I must confess that this particular path has been a large part of my own spiritual questing, especially in the past ten years or so. In addition to the other quotes from various sources in this chapter, let me then add three more to illustrate my point from a little book called *Oneness: Great Principles Shared by All Religions*, by Jeffrey Moses:

> *Do not search in distant skies for God.*
> *He is found in man's own heart.*
> Shintoism

> *God bides hidden in the hearts of all.*
> Hinduism

> *Why wilt thou go into the jungles?*
> *What do you hope to find there?*
> *Even as the scent dwells within the flower,*
> *so God within thine own heart ever abides.*
> *Seek Him with earnestness and find Him there.*
> Sikhism

But how do we pray to and with the God within? I don't know about you, but in all my years in Sunday school, church, and eventually an Anglican seminary, where I was later to go on and become a professor myself, I was never taught or even once told about such a possibility! In fact, in the low church, evangelical wing of Anglicanism (or Episcopalianism as it is known in the United States), in which I and my three siblings were later brought up, there was much more emphasis on our basic sinfulness and depravity than there ever was on the possibility of God already being present in our souls or "hearts." I was told to again accept Christ and "let him come in" instead of being helped to acknowledge the fact that all I had to do was to open my inner eye and realize God was already there waiting to be known and followed. We were taught little, if anything, about the great mystics and about the long tradition of meditation in our own Christian faith. In the next chapter, we will examine this kind of inner prayer in some detail. I strongly believe now that when Jesus spoke of going into "your room" and, after "shutting the door" to pray "in secret," he was talking about going within oneself. His saying about the Kingdom of God being within us has become a key part of my personal creed and a chief pillar supporting my experience of praying.

There is a remarkable passage in Herman Melville's classic novel *Moby Dick*, where the narrator, a whaler named Ishmael, is describing a whale hunt in which a vast number of pods of the animals have come together and are swimming about in utter panic and confusion. However, at the very center of this furious maelstrom, as in the eye of hurricane, there is a deep calm where the young frolic and bask in peace. As is his wont, Ishmael suddenly breaks off from his description into a reverie of his own thoughts and reflections. He becomes the author's own voice for a moment as he says, "But even so, amid the tornadoed Atlantic of my being, do I myself still forever centrally disport in mute calm; and while ponderous planets of unwaning woe revolve around me, deep down and deep inland there I still bathe me in eternal mildness of joy." That's precisely the experience we're talking about here.

FOOD FOR THOUGHT AND ACTION

Find a quiet place either indoors or out and try to calmly cultivate a sense of stillness. Have you ever or can you now recall a time when, through an experience of nature or of just being alone, you were aware of being one with something or Someone much greater than you have ever known before? Think about this for a little while. Imagine the experience once again, but completely internally. It may help to create a place or space in the center of your chest where this sense of being in the presence of Another can be re-created – visualize a favorite beach or holiday haunt, a forest or a waterfall, or perhaps a purling trout stream. Then, trusting and imagining that whatever you understand to be God is there with you, begin to talk silently as you would with a friend. Be sure to leave space for listening. Don't try too hard. In fact, relax as fully as you can. You are already well on the way.

V

INNER PRAYER AND MEDITATION

And Isaac went out to meditate in the field at the eventide.
Genesis 24:63 (KJV)

———

Let the words of my mouth
and the meditation of my heart
be acceptable to you, O Lord,
my rock and my redeemer.
Psalm 19:14

———

Be a light unto yourself.
Gautama Buddha

———————

*Mindfulness (meditation)…has everything to do with waking up
and living in harmony with oneself and with the world.
It has to do with examining who we are, with questioning our view
of the world and our place in it, and with cultivating
some appreciation of each moment of our lives.*
Jon Kabat-Zinn, *Wherever You Go, There You Are:
Mindfulness Meditation in Everyday Life*[1]

———————

*Where there is peace and meditation,
there is neither anxiety nor doubt.*
St. Francis of Assisi (c.1181–1226)

Any keen observer of the current scene knows that there are literally hundreds of books around today, both contemporary and revived from the near and more distant past, on the subject of meditation. Major religions such as Judaism and its much larger offspring, Christianity, are now in the throes of rediscovering their own meditation traditions. Ever since the Beatles went to visit the Maharishi Mahesh Yogi, sometimes called "the giggling Guru," in India in the early 1960s, Eastern meditation techniques have been popularized and are now firmly entrenched in our Western culture.

Secular meditation, or mind-training (awareness meditation based chiefly on the Buddhist model), is becoming more widely used by people trying to reverse heart disease – for example in the Dr. Dean Ornish heart disease reversal program – to combat chronic pain, insomnia, high blood pressure and other physical ills, and by millions of other ordinary folk who are more or less well but who are simply trying to find a focus of calm and of purpose for their lives. Secular meditation is currently being used in stress management clinics for corporate workaholics, in programs of stress reduction for the poor and for other minorities in the inner city, in therapy for prison inmates with addictive or violent behavior problems, and for professionals of all kinds from Olympic and professional athletes to judges and priests. Daily meditation, whether TM (Transcendental Meditation) or whatever, has a proven track record of lowering blood pressure, lifting mild depression and lessening anxiety.

At the same time, there is now a World Community for Christian Meditation – founded by Dom John Main, O.S.B. – with 200 associated groups in Canada alone. Similar communities exist in over 35 countries today. They use an Aramaic word from the New Testament, *Maranatha*, "Come, Lord" as their

mantra or focus of concentration. This mantra is repeated silently, that is to say, inwardly, with the eyes closed, for roughly 15
or 20 minutes twice a day. Other believers of various kinds (including myself from time to time), employ one or the other of
the Hebrew words, *Amen* or *Shalom*, as a mantra in meditation.
By repeating either of these, or some other valued term or phrase
softly within, in time with one's breathing, one can calm the
mind and express deep praise at the same time.

In what follows here, I want to try to simplify what can seem
like a remote or complex subject – one which for many people is
surrounded with mystery or with a possibly off-putting sort of
New Age aura. Mention meditation to some people and they
immediately imagine someone sitting crosslegged in an incense-
filled room, repeating the name of some hitherto unheard-of
deity, and then eating scented coriander seeds or some other
more exotic "treat." In essence, however, though there is indeed
a wide variety of schools and methods, meditation itself is a
fairly simple matter. It has as we have seen a long history in all
major religious traditions.

That's not to say it's easy, of course. Meditation requires
constant discipline and effort. The more secular sort focuses
on teaching one's mind (often called the "crazy monkey" by
Hindus) to stay alert, focused, in touch with life and with one's
deepest self. This is done through concentration on a mantra,
or on one's own breathing (the cool feeling against the back of
the nostrils as air comes in, and the warmth as it exits the
nostrils in a steady, slow rhythm), or through the use of mental
imagery, a light, a candle and so forth. The spiritual/religious
kind of meditation focuses on the Source of all being within
each person. It can be done either in silence or through use of
a beloved sacred phrase or other mantra (for example, a one-

word prayer such as *Shanti*, the Hindu term for peace). The aim of both secular and religious/spiritual meditation is to take time out from the world of "doing" in order to concentrate on the process of "being" and becoming. It's the practice of being fully, yet silently, locked in the here-and-now in order to transform both the present and future.

One could recommend Jon Kabat-Zinn's 1994 book *Wherever You Go, There You Are*, particularly for those who want to relieve stress and improve their general health but who don't necessarily feel a need for or want recourse to ideas about God, or to attempt to pray in the spiritual manner of a believer. It's not that Kabat-Zinn is opposed to faith or prayer. He certainly is not. His aim is to offer a tool to be used by nonbelievers and believers alike in order to increase general awareness and to calm both mind and body. However, as Dr. Herbert Benson of Harvard Medical School has now shown in his most recent research work, meditation which uses a sacred mantra or brief faith affirmation as its basic tool has verifiably better holistic health results overall than religiously neutral mantras or other techniques.[2]

Benson has recorded a series of experiments in which he invited certain participants to use a favorite faith word or words as their mantra or focus point for daily meditation: for example, The Lord is my Shepherd; or the Hebrew word for peace, Shalom; or the Arabic word for the same reality, Salaam. Of course, as he notes, the Indian words, Shanti (peace), or Om, believed to have been the sound of the primal vibration spoken by God at Creation, are equally appropriate. But so is any inspiring word, phrase, or brief prayer which is especially meaningful to you. The others in the control group either used a secular term or no mantra at all. Benson found that the benefits scientifically recorded in his previous books *The Relaxation Response* and *Be-*

yond the Relaxation Response, which were based on such secular-type meditation, were significantly surpassed when a meaningful faith affirmation or word was added.

In any case, if you really want to cultivate the inner conversation with God I spoke of in the previous chapter, if you want to grow in prayer as you learn more of "the God within," you have to know and experience more of the meditative way than you ever have in the past. That's my own experience anyway. Like Bishop "Honest to God" Robinson whom we met in the introduction, I too have known what it is like not to be on the prayer train one is supposed to be on as "a committed Christian" and an Anglican priest. (They're not necessarily the same thing!) As I hinted earlier, I never did find saying the Anglican Prayer Book "Office" of daily Morning Prayer, in addition to an even earlier "Quiet Time" of one's own at bedside in the chill of dawn (much favored by evangelicals and others) very conducive to effective or relevant praying during my student or clerical days. I was always too sleepy at the first crack of dawn. The sense of obligation, together with the appallingly dry sameness of the various *Prayer Book* rituals (in spite of their antique eloquence and beauty), ruined morning chapel for me during ten years of university, nine of them spent in residence where daily services were mandatory, and seven years of seminary teaching (again I lived in the college) where the same routine was followed.

SOME PERSONAL EXAMPLES

I did eventually develop my own style of prayer life which saw me long ago dropping all "thee's" and "thou's" and other formalities for plain talk and regarding any place as just as fit for praying as a church, synagogue, temple, or other sacred building. Most pleasant of all, I learned how to pray while

walking. Walking and hiking are among my most favorite
allurements and always have been. For example, as I noted in
Chapter two, I have walked five miles each morning before
going to my desk to write for the past 18 years. That represents a good deal of time, perhaps more than most can muster. But, thanks to learning how to use it in part for praying,
either aloud or silently, and for meditation, it has become
what is now called in the literature a "double-dip" occasion.
Body and soul get renewed or built up simultaneously. I have
found that the inspiration for writing books or columns truly
begins to flow because of – and often during – this time of
prayer-meditation and exercise.

In recent years, I have increasingly felt the need to go much
further in prayer. So, as I have already hinted, I have been experimenting more for some time now with various forms of
meditation or inner conversation/contemplation. For example,
I now find that silently repeating the word "Amen" (so be it),
in a steady rhythm with one's breathing and walking pace at
the same time, can effectively calm, clear, and focus the mind
for further prayer or – just generally – for the day ahead. The
same is true for me of the word Shalom, used as a mantra as I
walk. As I breathe in, I try to invoke peace and justice for my
own life. On the outbreath, I send it forth prayerfully to loved
ones, my community, or the particular part of the world most
in my thoughts at that time. Another favorite mantra for me is
the line from the 23rd Psalm: "I will not fear, for you are with
me." Sometimes I shorten this to simply, "You are with me." I
say a word of this phrase each time my left foot hits the road
and soon it becomes almost unconscious. Similarly with the
breath. Sometimes, I simply inhale on one beat of the left foot
and exhale on the next as well.

I invite you to experiment with this, creating your own mantra and breathing patterns or rhythms either while walking alone or while seated upright in a place at home or outdoors that you have set apart as your "quiet place." But above all, take a very relaxed approach to all of it and feel totally free to adapt or invent a method which suits and makes the most sense to you and your particular lifestyle. I am not personally very taken with any of the rigid schools of thought or techniques applied to prayer. They tend to impede rather than advance the cause, in my view. It would certainly disappoint me if readers were to use only whatever speaks to them in this book – unless they remember always to do so *in their own way*.

But certainly, if you have never tried it before and if you are really keen to move forward in your prayer life, I would suggest that you begin to pray and/or meditate while walking. "Walking Prayer" – conversing with God as your friend and companion, or in simple, silent mindfulness of the Divine Presence in and around and through the whole of nature and your own being – will bring a reality and an intimacy to your praying that will take you far beyond all the distant, superficial and boringly repetitive prayers of the past.

Incidently, if you spend a lot of time in your car or on public transportation – including travel by air – you can make excellent use of these sometimes "wasted" hours by spending a part of them in silent prayer or meditation. In the case of driving, if you are alone, it can be a great opportunity to pray aloud. I have found that it's safer – so much easier to keep your mind and eyes fully on your driving – if you can voice your petitions or praise rather than internalize them. One slight caution: you may have to put all this on hold at stop signs, or in very slow traffic. If there is another car or cars beside you, you could risk being thought a little eccentric!

LISTENING

In all of this I have said very little about the listening aspect of relating to God's presence within. You don't necessarily need to use mantras, or other sacred phrases, or to spend all your prayer time telling God your problems, thanksgivings, or requests. Seat yourself on a fairly firm chair, sitting comfortably but upright. Feel the floor beneath your feet. Feel the chair beneath your buttocks and at your back. Then, breathe quietly for a while, paying attention to your breath, focusing on the tip of your nose or just inside your nostrils. Relax as much as you can. Then, just let all thoughts and emotions slip gently away. You will still have thoughts flitting in and out, but just keep gently bringing your focus back to the breath. Tell yourself that God – using whatever name you call the Source and Spirit beneath, through, and under all things – is within you now. It may help to locate this Presence in your chest area, close to or actually within your heart. The heart, as is well said, is so much more than a pump! You can visualize, as I sometimes do, a gorgeous cathedral, mosque or shrine inside. It far surpasses Chartres, Canterbury Cathedral, Salisbury, or St. Peter's Basilica in Rome. And there is a spring of clear water welling up before the altar and flowing in a channel down the main aisle to become a stream outdoors. You, of course, may have quite another hallowed place, a holy cave, or a fantastic landscape in your imagination.

In any case, my practice is to put myself within that scene and just sit silently, alert and waiting and listening. I do not hear any voices or see any visions myself. Many people, however, perhaps holier or more sensitive, report a whole range of mystical experiences during such times, from a sense of mystical one-ness with all things to an inner instructor who offers guidance along the way. My own sense of "hearing" God's voice comes, rather, from a range of "hunches" or "intuitions" which seem to arise out of nowhere at such times yet which carry considerable authority. Usually, they throw at least some light on projects, problems or personalities with which I am currently dealing. I don't regard these "messages" as infallible, because I know from experience that it's very easy to get carried away, to suppose that what seems to have been "spoken" is inevitably always the will or mind of God. The "crazy monkey" of the mind, already re-ferred to, doesn't stop acting up just because we are meditating. There is a real need afterwards to think about the information or ideas given as I listened. I ask God for wisdom and a sense of discernment in evaluating the "messages." I check them with conscience, with further reflection, and often with my wife and other insightful friends. Nevertheless, having made this process public, I must say that this regular practice has become deeply meaningful and helpful in my life. Prayer, especially in recent years, has become a two-way street instead of an often peevish-sounding, self-centered monologue.

AN OPPORTUNITY TO RESPOND

1. Try a little inner review and stock-taking. Are you still stuck
   with concepts and practices of prayer which you learned long
   ago and which have become stale or limiting to you today?
   Surprising as it may seem, millions of people who pray are
   still repeating the simple, often totally self-centered prayers
   they learned at their mother's knee. In my research I have
   interviewed a lot of people who have no qualms about saying their idea of prayer is to repeat word for word whatever it
   was they learned as children, including my least favorite
   children's prayer: "Now I lay me down to sleep..." Have you
   ever directed your prayers inwardly instead of outwardly to a
   God-in-the-skies? Take one of the ideas just set out regarding meditation and, adapting it as you see fit, try it regularly –
   twice a day if possible for at least ten minutes at a time. Keeping a very simple diary of your experience will help you see
   that you are making progress, even though it may be quite
   hesitant and brief at first. Try to find even a very few minutes
   a day when you keep silent and listen for what God has to say
   to you.

2. Decide on an inspiring word, phrase or scripture verse to use
   as a mantra or prayer focus. The important thing to remember is that it has to "fit" your personality and needs. I find it
   helpful to have several mantras and to use them according to
   my particular mood or problem on any given day. Others
   recommend you have only one or two and use them for a
   week or so at a time. I stress again the importance of choosing what works best for you.

VI

PRAYERS
WITH "SUCTION"

The real problem with most people's prayers
is that they ain't got no suction!
From a sermon on "real praying," by the minister of a black holiness church,
near Freeport, in the Bahamas, January, 1989

My God, My God, why have you forsaken me?
Why are you so far from helping me,
From the words of my groaning?
O my God, I cry by day, but you do not answer;
And by night, but find no rest.

Psalm 22:1ff

———

Pray as if you were to die tomorrow.

Benjamin Franklin (1706–1790)

From *Poor Richard's Almanac*, May 1757

The Pentecostal black preacher in the Bahamas, quoted above, gave us a sermon to remember for a long time. He said most of our prayers have about as much passion to them as a kiss on the cheek from a great-aunt or from an aged grandparent on one's 21st birthday; they lack suction. For him, lack of suction was a metaphor for an overly polite, even rather embarrassed, shallow, passionless effort at communication with God. He couldn't have been more right. Most of our attempts at prayer, apart from formal worship which presents its own set of barriers, are almost totally lacking in depth, genuine honesty, or fervor of any kind. For much, if not most of our lives, our prayers lack the spontaneity, warmth and frankness normal in any deep conversation or relationship with friends, relatives or lovers. Rarely do we pray as though we were about to die tomorrow. Small wonder, then, that our prayers thus tend to become boring, flat, unable to move our own soul or to facilitate an experience of contact with anything or Anyone beyond ourselves. We become praying automatons.

This is not meant to imply that the mystery we call God is somehow moved or persuaded to act on our behalf in direct proportion to the amount of emotion and of intense repetition we can generate in our praying. As part of his lead-up or introduction to the Lord's Prayer in the Sermon on the Mount, Matthew quotes Jesus as saying, "When you are praying, do not heap up empty phrases as the Gentiles do; for they think they will be heard because of their many words. Do not be like them; for your Father knows what you need before you ask him" (Matthew 6:7–8).

That entire model of a reluctant Deity being won over by our eloquence or passion is wrong and unhelpful in any case. Prayers with "suction" can just as well be moments in which we

use no words at all. As noted already, sometimes our prayers are
what Paul in his Letter to the Romans calls, "inarticulate cries"
or groanings which can't be uttered. He says that there are "sighs
too deep for words" which the Spirit utters within us, interced-
ing on our behalf. In other words, the crisis we or others dear to
us may be going through can be too overwhelming or complex
for any words to describe. "We do not know how to pray as we
ought," as Paul puts it (Romans 8:26–27), and so we are left
with nothing but "the sound of silence."

But just as there can be a deep silence between friends or
lovers which communicates deep love, understanding, or tremendous support much better than mere words can do, so too
with the deepest prayer. When we feel the urge to pray but can't
find the "right words" – there are never any "right words" when
conversing with God anyway – then a deep silence is not only
enough, it is the best mode of all. The intention is there. The
direction of the soul is set passionately towards the Ultimate.
That is enough. The "suction" is there if the longing for contact
and for the Divine Will to be done in our lives or in any other
particular situation is genuine enough, profound enough, filled
with honesty, and truly flowing from the core of our being.

THE POWER OF PRAYER

In my own life, I am aware that most, if not all, that I have
learned about prayer with passion or "suction" has come not
from books about praying or from preachers who are eloquent
on the topic. It has come from my own experience over the
years, especially when wrestling with what to me is in many
ways the most profound and moving writing in the entire Bible,
Hebrew or Christian. I'm referring to the Psalter, or Book of
Psalms, from which I have already quoted many times.

The Psalms are not a religious or pious treatise on this subject; much better, they're a supreme example of what prayers with "suction" actually feel, look, and sound like. In them, we have left theory far behind and are in the immediate world of practical, day-to-day living. They are, and always have been, treasured (for so many centuries) by millions of Jews, Christians, Muslims and a host of others of no religion at all. When it comes to genuine prayer, the Psalms don't talk about it, they do it. The various authors of the Psalter have left for us the most intimate "soul diary" or "prayer diary" possible. They have let everything "hang out" so to speak. A thousand times better than having someone expound on any topic is to actually see the activity or process being described already at work in somebody's life. In the Psalms, that's what has been given to us. We see prayer boldly expressed in real situations – and all through the lens of a candid camera.

There is, for example, no attempt to "cozy up" to God or the Great Spirit. There is no sense of an anemic, cautious, timid approach. As we saw earlier in the case of the so-called Lord's Prayer, the tone is at times almost scary in its bluntness and honesty. The true feelings of the person praying in the Psalms, as opposed to his thoughts or rationalizations, are always up front and center. In each case, he prays in the certainty of his inherent right to a hearing and to an answer. In other words, the prayers are made as very direct requests or even demands to a parent-type Reality around him and within. I'm reminded of what I once read somewhere about adopted children. You can tell they're beginning to feel secure and a real part of their adoptive family when they begin to complain, when they begin to feel they have some rights or legitimate expectations. That's the way the psalmist seems to feel.

As you read them, and if, as I did, you come from a fairly traditional religious background, you will probably be quite startled at first at how often the question "why?" is angrily hurled in God's face. For example, in Psalm 43, written in a time of deep anguish, the author calls boldly on God to deliver him from an unjust situation:

> *For you are the God in*
> *whom I take refuge;*
> *why have you cast me off?*
> *Why must I walk about*
> *mournfully*
> *because of the oppression of the enemy?*
> Psalm 43:2

Psalm 64 begins, "Hear my voice, O God, in my complaint; preserve my life from the dread enemy..."

Psalm 42 has often been a natural part of praying for me in times of difficulty. The psalm is a favorite of mine, as it is, of course, of many. You have to love the frankness of the author as he interrogates both God and his own inner, higher self. We have as it were a wide window directly into his soul. First he tells God about his longing for a taste of the Divine Presence. His soul "thirsts for God." Then, he complains, "When shall I come and behold the face of God?" There is both anger at and a sad rebuke of God as he fleshes out his uncertainty and pain:

> *My tears have been my food*
> *day and night,*
> *while people say to me continually,*
> *"Where is your God?"*
> Psalm 42:3

He then goes on to remind God that he has been a frequent worshipper at the temple; he has, in fact, taken a leading role in encouraging "the throng" to attend "the house of God" and to observe with joy the various festivals of praise. But then he says that if, in fact, all this is true,

> *Why are you cast down*
> *O my soul,*
> *and why are you disquieted*
> *within me?*
> Psalm 42:5

He believes he has done his part and that it's now time for God to take notice and respond.

As the psalm progresses, the fascinating give-and-take of the dialogue between his innermost being and God is a form of highest drama. He moves between affirmations of hope and trust and almost petulant arguments in which he points out that in spite of his promises God seems to have been ignoring him. "Why have you forgotten me?" he cries in verse nine.

I cannot tell you how often and with what difficulty, throughout the years of my formal ministry within the structures of the Anglican Church, I have had to try to persuade staid members of my flock – who were going through some similar kind of mental, emotional, spiritual or physical hell as the psalmists report – to get their anger against God out on the table. Most traditionally minded religious people of all faiths have a tremendous problem here. Timidity and/or a false politeness force them to keep up a hypocritical facade in praying. As a result, nothing real seems to happen. True, they have avoided facing their own repressed wrath and the risk of offending [sic] their

God.Yet they're also left feeling like they're trying to water the lawn with a hose but no water is coming out. Although their intentions are clear and everything looks normal, they're un-aware that there's a knot in the hose somewhere or that they're actually standing on it themselves. Often, the strain of keeping the anger hidden is too much and results in severe depression or other illness.

For people in deep depression, facing extreme grief over the death of a loved one, or the harsh message that they them-selves have an incurable disease – or any other tragedy in their lives – we know that anger against life, the universe, or God is a profound, almost immediate reaction. Instead of recognizing how natural this is and expressing it in prayers, whether verbal or "inarticulate cries," it often seems easier to repress it or uncon-sciously project it on others – doctors, family members, or whom-ever. In most cases, the anger is turned back inside, and because it doesn't feel safe to vent it against God, we use it as a whip to flog our already damaged soul. Our prayers, because not founded on truth, seem to mock us.The deep bitterness of soul too often grows accordingly.

The Psalms have taught me that it is not only safe but an extremely important duty and therapy to tell God about how angry and fed-up we really feel at certain junctures. Christ him-self provides the supreme example of this when, hanging from the cross, he utters the words of Psalm 22, with its haunting cry of anguish and anger:"Why have you forsaken me, O God?" If, as I believe, God is the source and ground of very being, and of the entire cosmos, then he is more than capable of hearing and absorbing our wrath. It's significant, I believe, that the most honest and in a way most shocking communication with God in the whole of the Bible, the "why have you forsaken me" cry of dereliction from the cross, comes from one of the Psalms. Significant also is the fact that although this particular psalm is an almost clinical description of someone going through the darkest possible night of the soul (a severe depression), it ends on the highest possible note of loving faith and hope (verses 22 to the end). The reader of the Gospel of Matthew is meant to understand from the context (Matthew 27:45ff) that Jesus quoted the entire psalm as he hung on the cross.

The overall thrust here is simple enough; it's also *crucial*, especially if we want our prayers to transcend what they have been in the past, if we want to make progress in the spiritual life, if we long to discover that our petitions and intimate conversations with the Divine can indeed move from the anemic and the formal to something solid and down-to-earth – to something with a true "suction" on our lives. Pour your real self into your prayers. Hold nothing back, particularly those thoughts, feelings or actions of which you are ashamed and would like to keep as unconscious as possible. Pray aloud if and when you can – perhaps, as suggested before, in the car or on a long walk. Use the most simple, direct language you know, the kind you use with close associates or in your own inner dialogue with yourself. And, when you can't think of what to say or how to say it, tell God so and keep silent. Remain open to God speaking to you. Prayer as we have seen is not just an "I talk, you listen" kind of arrangement. God will "speak" to you, not in some loud voice coming down from Sinai but in the still small voice of inner intuitions and soul-promptings. There is no time and no situation in which one cannot pray. That's why one ancient expert on prayer, the Apostle Paul (or an associate, depending on your view of who wrote the letters to Timothy), was able to tell some early Christians to "pray without ceasing." In his Letter to the

Philippians, Paul says, "In everything, by prayer and supplication with thanksgiving, let your requests be made known unto God..." (Philippians 4:6).

Notice the tiny rider clause the apostle slips in almost casually – "with thanksgiving." I have written elsewhere at some length about the great importance of deepening one's growing spirituality by giving thanks. But it would be impossible to say too much about it. I like Sir John Templeton's advice for beginning each day. The amazingly successful investment expert, who has now retired from his multimillion dollar trust funds to spend his entire time promoting research and progress in the realm of spiritual programs and ideas, recently told a packed meeting of the Canadian Club in Toronto his personal recipe for life: "I make it my practice to begin each and every day – often even before getting out of bed – by listing five things for which I have deep cause to be thankful. It has made all the difference."

As you reread the Psalms to see how to truly wrestle with God in prayers with suction, notice not just the honesty regarding anger, resentment, and complaints. Pay close attention as well to just how much time and space is given over to passionate outpourings of praise, gratitude and sheer joy at what God has done, is doing, and will do in the days to come. The delight and awe at God's handiwork in the heavens above or the oceans below – throughout the whole of creation – has enormous power to suction out any bitterness or needless preoccupation with self. For example:

The heavens are telling the glory of God;
and the firmament
proclaims his handiwork.

Day to day pours forth
speech,
and night to night declares
knowledge...
Psalm 19:1ff

Prayers with "suction" include a deepening appreciation of the multiplicity of things each one of us has reason to be truly grateful for. How can God grant our most urgent petitions while we are so concerned about our present needs that we fail to notice "what the Lord has done" already? Profound thankfulness for answered prayers and for "all the blessings of this life" is a form of soul-conditioning that helps us realize that the God who has been there for us in the past is still with us and "for us" now and in any conceivable future. I am reminded of an incident involving a hitchhiker I saw last summer who was thumbing a ride on the Trans-Canada Highway, in the interior of British Columbia. The hitchhiker was so intent on watching the oncoming traffic that he failed to notice that a car had already stopped to pick him up and was waiting for him some distance ahead on a narrow shoulder of the road. The "answer" he was so keenly seeking was already in place, but he had no time or eyes to see it. Eventually, the driver tired of the delay and slipped back into the traffic again. Strange to say, the hiker was still looking earnestly the other way as his ride disappeared around a distant curve.

Now, most of the above has come from a Jewish or Christian context, but the principles described apply to all religions as well as to secular-type praying outside the scope of any faith whatever. Let me close, then, with a Hindu prayer that fulfills the qualification for true prayers given by the black preacher in the Bahamas with whom I began.

> *May Brahman (God) protect us,*
> *May he guide us,*
> *May he give us strength and right understanding.*
> *May love and harmony be with us all.*
> *OM...Peace – Peace – Peace.*
>
> The Upanishads – *Breath of the Eternal*

FOR PRACTICAL ACTION RIGHT NOW

1. Whatever your faith or your lack of one, resolve now to read through the Psalms paying particular attention to the honesty and informality of the various speakers. Look for the differences between how you pray, if and when you do, and how the authors express themselves. Experiment with praying more like them.

2. Take time for a little reflection on the biggest issues facing you at this moment — whether they concern your health, your work, your relationships, or any other crises or fears. As you do this, look for the anger lurking underneath. Is there indeed anger? Does it, as you look at it truthfully, have anything to do with your real feelings about the ultimate mystery we call "God"? Write down — for your eyes only — what this anger is about and how it really makes you feel. Then, pour it out to God verbally or nonverbally and feel yourself embraced by acceptance, forgiveness and a fresh empowerment to carry on. In some cases, the anger — and the guilt we feel about it — will fade away almost instantly. For others, especially if the repression of it has gone on for many years, it will be a longer, more gradual process. We are not talking about magic here. But I can promise you from my own experience and my direct observation of so many others that there will be definite, discernible changes for the better and, eventually, a "closer walk with God" than ever before.

PART THREE

GETTING
PERSONAL

Thus says the Lord who made you,
who formed you in the womb and will help you:
Do not fear…
Isaiah 44:2

VII

PRAYERS FOR PERSONAL ADAPTATION

*All you **big** things, bless the Lord*
Mount Kilimanjaro and Lake Victoria
The Rift Valley and the Serengeti Plain
Fat baobabs and shady mango trees
All eucalyptus and tamarind trees
Bless the Lord
Praise and extol Him for ever and ever.

*All you **tiny** things, bless the Lord*
busy black ants and hopping fleas
Wriggling tadpoles and mosquito larvae
Flying locusts and water drops
Pollen dust and tsetse flies
Millet seeds and dried dagaa
Bless the Lord
Praise and extol Him for ever and ever.

J. Carden, "An African Canticle"[1]

O Lord, support us all the day long, until the shadows lengthen
and the evening comes, and the busy world is hushed,
and our work is done. Then, in thy mercy,
grant us a safe lodging, and a holy rest,
and peace at the last. Amen.

Adapted from the Anglican *Book of Common Prayer*

———

How long, O lord?
Will you forget me forever?
How long will you hide your face from me?
How long must I bear pain in my soul,
and have sorrow in my heart all day long?

Psalm 13:1–2

We have seen how a prayer can be a phrase of a few informal words, even a one- or two-word exclamation; it can be "uttered" in no words at all, or in sighs too deep to be verbalized. It can also consist of sincere intentions, in work done for others, or even in work simply done well for its own sake. The ancient Latin motto of the Benedictine Order, founded by the "Patriarch of Western Monasticism," St. Benedict of Nursia (c.480–c.550 CE), is *Orare est laborare, laborare est orare*, which means, "To pray is to work, to work is to pray." On the other hand, prayer can also be "set," as in formal or "official" prayer, and often of considerable length, as in the Christian Service of Holy Communion, also known as the Eucharist or Mass. It can range all the way from the most spontaneous outpourings made anywhere, to the lengthy, prepared "pastoral" prayers offered in many Protestant churches by the minister each Sunday.

Personally, I think that the person prays best who strives to pray earnestly and with total honesty from his or her own heart, letting the inner Spirit guide regarding length, language (or absence of it), and intention. At the same time, it can help a lot, especially at the beginning, to have some written models to look at and perhaps to adapt for one's own use. This is a temporary measure, of course, and if you are already well along on the path of prayer, the following prayers, originally composed for my own use, can simply be read and then put on one side for further reference. Obviously, it would be foolish to make a pretense of trying to cover the gamut of occasions and issues for which conversation with God is both instinctual and necessary. But these prayers can point the way and make a solid beginning for the serious seeker.

AT THE START OF THE DAY

Divine Spirit, thanks for today, for life and strength renewed, and for the rest and sleep of the past night. (Sometimes, as Sir John Templeton recommends, I go on to list here five special things for which I'm very thankful at this moment of my journey.) *I don't know completely what this day holds in store for me and for those closest to me. But you know and understand. Go before us and keep us true to your will and safe from harm to body, soul and spirit. Help us to be continually conscious of your presence and guidance in all we think and feel and do. May we have the wisdom and compassion we need to be channels of your love and light in the world. I ask this just for today. Amen.*

IN THE EVENING

Lord of Light, far beyond the shining of the sun, now that evening has come again and Earth grows dark, I thank you for the great gift of this day. Bless all that was good in it and forgive my weaknesses and my mistakes, particularly...(specifics).

I hold up in the presence of your Divine Light the following loved ones and others who are in need of special healing and/or blessing. (Name individual[s] and briefly imagine them bathed in the Light of God's Presence.) *I remember before you all those who are in any kind of trouble – gripped by fear, illness, grief, poverty or hunger. Please give us all a quiet night, sound sleep, and health and strength renewed for tomorrow.*

IN MOMENTS OF NEED FOR CALMNESS AND GUIDANCE THROUGHOUT THE DAY

O God, right now I'm feeling anxious and afraid. This problem (name the situation, task or other challenge) *is too daunting. I don't quite know what to do next. I ask for help to calm down, to do my best, with you beside me and within. With you, I know, all things are possible. So I'm claiming this as your promise to me now. I'm going forward aware that I'm not alone. I will fear no evil for you are with me indeed. Thank you. Amen.*

WHEN MOVED BY BEAUTY IN NATURE, MUSIC, OR ELSEWHERE

Creator Spirit, my whole inner being is full of joy and wonder at the great beauty of the Earth, at the skies and the knowledge of uncounted galaxies beyond (for the color of the autumn woods, or for this inspired piece of music, or for the glimpse of glory afforded by this painting, etc.). *At times such as this, my heart and soul are more alive and aware of your presence than at any other moment. Thank you for the vastness of scale, the gorgeous simplicity, and at the same time the mind-numbing complexity of all creation; for flowers, birds and animals; and for the presence and talents of other people. All my worries and petty concerns now fall away and I forget them as I am lost in awe and praise. Thank you, thank you, for everything.*

IN SUDDEN PAIN OR ANXIETY

Divine Light, within me and without, come now and flood my mind, my imagination, my emotions, and my entire body with your healing presence. You are the source of wholeness, health and peace. You know my every thought and need. You have not given us a spirit of fear but a spirit "of power, of love, and of a sound mind." Chase the darkness of my present fears.

Enter this situation in power yet great gentleness. Make me aware again of the promises of God to be with us no matter where we go or whatever it is we must endure. Help me to do your will in this moment and in all things. At the same time, please help my unbelief, God. Amen.

FOR A FRIEND OR LOVED ONE IN ILLNESS OR OTHER DIFFICULTY

Great Spirit of Love, of Power and Might, I hold up (name[s]) in the light of your presence. Often, I don't really know how to pray for them because I don't know all about their situation, and, even if I did, I lack the wisdom to know for certain what would truly be for the best. But you see behind and before. You know their needs, their innermost hearts and their commitments to others beyond. Bless them, I pray. Deliver them from this affliction or trial by your great grace, and according to your will. Restore them in perfect wholeness to those who love them and grant that they, being healed, may once again serve you in everything they think and do. Amen.

FOR PERSONAL GROWTH AND FOR COURAGE ON THE JOURNEY

God, often the road seems hard and my progress on the spiritual path seems minimal or painfully slow at best. Sometimes I feel lazy and I long for more comfortable ways. Sometimes I fear the cost, the obstacles to be overcome, the thorns in the flesh to be endured, the ceaseless effort.

It's so tempting for all of us to become discouraged. But I know that none of your prophets or seers ever said it would be easy. I realize there is no true victory in any field that is wholly free from pain. So I ask for the courage to keep walking, putting one foot ahead of the other, not heeding any of the negative "voices" either from inside me or from without.

Help me daily to grow into your Light. Increase my self-discipline, my compassion, and my inner wisdom that I may be increasingly a channel for that Light. In Christ's name, I ask it.

FOR GREATER COMPASSION

Great Spirit of Love and of Mercy to all humankind – and especially to me – I am conscious at times of not having moved very far along the road of compassion for others. It's so often much simpler to be judgmental of them instead – never meaning to be so, of course – and to condemn rather than to encourage and support them.

Open my eyes both to my own faults and frailties and to the handicaps and hurdles faced by those I'm so often quick to criticize. Above all, open my heart to all the hidden suffering and need around me. Help me to feel this pain and to show compassion in ways that really mean something – in my attitudes, my words, and, above all, in new and solid acts of loving, practical solidarity with them. Amen.

FOR VICTIMS OF CATASTROPHES, WARS, FAMINES, PLAGUES, OR MASSIVE EXPLOITATION AT HOME OR OVERSEAS

God our Father and Mother, sometimes it seems that reading the newspaper or watching the news is too overwhelming to bear. There is so much agony and suffering in the world, so much innocent pain endured, that I cannot understand. Like millions, I alternate at times between wanting to cry out in anger against you and giving way to a grief too great to be endured let alone expressed. The "mystery of evil," especially of the innocent suffering, seems too complex and vast even to wrestle with. I pray, however, for this particular group (earthquake victims, torrents of refugees, survivors of terrorist attacks, or whomsoever the tragedy has struck). *Surround them with your mercy and comfort, deliver them out of their terrors, hardships and griefs, and strengthen all those politicians, agencies, volunteers and others who are trying so hard to give them aid. Help me to see and do my part with not only prayer but also hard cash or other practical means, if required. Lord, have mercy on them and on us all.*

FOR THE RETURN OF ONE'S OWN HEALTH

O God, you who are the spring from which all healing and wholeness continually flow, I ask for a swift return to health of my body, mind and spirit.

I have gained some useful insights into my own shortcomings and strengths during this time of suffering. My ultimate trust in your nearness and goodness has been made stronger even though, at times, I have felt as though "your face has been hidden from me." I have learned how to receive from others and not always to be set on sticking with the giving side.

But enough is enough. I long to have full recovery. Raise me up, I ask, in newness of life and make my restored wellness a blessing in my work and on behalf of others both known to me and unknown. I long to be able to pray with the psalmist:

> *Bless the Lord, O my soul,*
> *and all that is within me,*
> *Bless his holy name.*
> *Bless the Lord, O my soul,*
> *and do not forget all his benefits —*
> *who forgives all your iniquity,*
> *who heals all your diseases...*
> Psalm 103:1–3

Lord, hear my prayer and let my cry come unto you. So be it. Amen.

FOR A LOVED ONE WHO IS TERMINALLY ILL

Dear God, our lives and times are always in your hands. Though our futures are hidden from us, you know the hour of our departure from this plane of life and the time of our coming home. We pray very

specially now for our mother (sister, husband, child) who is danger-
ously ill and close to death. Whether or not she is fully conscious or in
any way aware that we are here praying and caring doesn't really
matter. She can still know within that "The eternal God is our refuge
and underneath are the everlasting arms."

We commit her now to your profound love and mercy. Comfort
her and shed your light upon her as you lead her through the "valley
of the shadow." Be with us in our deep grief, our impending loss, and
in our sense of final helplessness. We believe that she will be wholly
safe and at peace in your presence and that we shall surely meet again
one day. We believe. Please help our often simultaneous unbelief. Amen.

FOR HELP IN FORGIVING SOMEONE

Creator Spirit, you who led Jesus of Nazareth both to challenge us to
forgive our enemies and to tell Peter to forgive a fellow disciple who
"sins against me" not seven times but "seventy-seven times" – a seemingly unlimited forgiveness – I have a real problem. I can't bring
myself to forgive my friend even once for his current attitude and what
he has done.

The truth is I'm finding that this forgiveness business is one of
the hardest spiritual commands of all. How can I get to forgiving my
enemies when I can't even seem to forgive a former friend?

Yet I know from previous, and yes, rare occasions when forgiveness has seemed to flow a little more easily, it's the only road to take in
the end. It really improves and changes how I feel in a very dramatic
way, not to mention the other party, and, when I think about it, I have
never afterwards once regretted practicing it.

So help me once again on this, Lord. Help me to see my friend
with your eyes and to realize how alike we really are; help me to be
quite honest about my part in provoking this conflict of wills in the
first place.

Grant me the courage, and the grace, even if I still believe I'm in the right this time, to forgive him freely. I know how generously I myself have been forgiven by you in the past and how much I will likely continue to need this in the balance of my life. Please help me to seek out and make this reconciliation happen, both for his sake and also for my own.

FOR FORGIVENESS FOR ONESELF

Loving and gracious God, you are the source of all mercy and forgiveness. I know I have erred against my brothers and sisters and against you by being basically dishonest or unfair about (some specific unpleasant episode). *I come to you now in sadness, not to make excuses or to minimize my fault, but to confess it and to say how truly sorry I am. I want to follow your will, but self-will, pride, anger and all the rest of it cause me to slip up time and again – and often it's almost over before I'm even aware it's happening. With your aid, I can do better, much better.*

Help me to see clearly how I can avoid this particular weakness or failure (losing one's temper, shirking a particular duty, trying to control others, overeating, or whatever) *and minimize the hurt to others. With your assistance and goodness, I am resolved not to repeat this mistake again in the future.*

Thank you for the assurance that forgiveness is always there for those who honestly repent and change their direction. Thank you that I am even now a forgiven person myself. Strengthen me as I try to make amends to those I have wronged. Amen.

HOW TO FIND THE RIGHT PATH IN
MAJOR LIFE DECISIONS

You who are to me both the Father of Light and the Mother of Infinite Compassion, I have a key decision to make regarding my future. I know I don't have to explain all the details and range of choices because they are all already known to you. What I greatly need just now is clarity of thinking, sensitivity of feeling or intuition, and openness to the promptings of your Spirit within.

Illumine my thoughts, I pray, and show me the path I should take. I'm not asking for a vision or some voice in my head telling me what to do. But I do believe you want the best for my life and that if I pay attention closely I will "hear" you guiding me.

In the past, sometimes you have spoken through wise friends or in strange synchronicities of events to show the way. Help me to have the gift of true discernment so that I can ignore the promptings of my lower self, the ego or "the monkey mind," and know when something from a deeper source, the Inner Light, my own or from others, is being communicated.

I truly want to do the right thing, the thing you will to have me do, the thing my God-given sense of deepest desire ultimately longs for. Be with me, then, as I decide and use the decision for your glory.

FOR ACCEPTANCE OF THE DEATH OF A LOVED ONE

God, you who are my rock and my refuge in times of trouble and distress, my whole being is drowning in shock, and in a terrible sadness — a sense of bereftness such as I have never known before. I am filled with conflicting feelings of anger, of bewilderment, and, yes, of guilt as well.

I know my mother is gone from this life, yet part of me can not, does not, accept that this is so. I can't imagine life without her, but it's already begun, and it seems as though it will be endless, and meaningless as well.

Please come to my aid and help me to know that you have not left me also. Help me to visualize her as surrounded by the light of your eternal Presence, fulfilled and happy. The only thought that makes this

*bearable in any way is that she is now free from all pain and released to
be her true self before you.*

*Help me to accept and to make some sort of sense out of what has
happened. Help me to keep going on in the faith that one day we two
shall meet once more in your supreme Light, where, as T. S. Eliot once put
it, "all shall be well and all manner of thing shall be well." Amen.*

FOR RELIEF FROM ANXIETY AND DEPRESSION

O God, you are my God,
I seek you,
my soul thirsts for you;
my flesh faints for you,
as in a dry and weary land
where there is no water."

Psalm 63:1

*These words express exactly how I feel, O God. It seems that a great,
dark dryness has swept my soul and that there are a multitude of fears
and anxieties outside me and within. I don't feel like praying at all. I
am at a loss to describe accurately what is happening or how I really
feel. But you know.*

*Sleep evades me or no longer refreshes. My body is racked by
pains of every kind and there are digestive problems – what I've read
doctors sometimes call "the organ recital." I know I have not always
cared for my body as I should have done; but the underlying problem
here seems to me to be an inner or spiritual one, not physical in origin.
I guess my body must simply be manifesting what my mind/soul
thinks and feels.*

*I pray for light in the midst of this darkness, for a deeper trust and
acceptance in the moments of anxiety or even, at times, of despair. I take*

heart and hope in the sure knowledge that you have delivered me from times and feelings like these in the past.

Hear my groanings and complaint and lift me "up from the desolate pit, out of the miry bog, and set my feet upon a rock, making my steps secure." May I soon be able to say, as the psalmist declared during a similar affliction, "He put a new song in my mouth, a song of praise to our God" (Psalm 40:2–3).

My trust is in you alone. Show me once more the light of your "countenance" and deliver me, I pray.

FOR STILLNESS

We are so needlessly busy most of the time, Lord, that it's hard to sit still, to be still, and to know quietness within. The result is much inner turmoil, a sense of rush or pressure, a failure to pray.

O God of the calm lake in the morning, the silent forest, the distant, misty mountains, the billions of soundless stars – and a million other scenes in nature of total peace and calm – help us, help me, just to sit still. Help us to imagine some enchanted place of utter quiet and beauty and to be still in it.

Grant us your peace, your still, small voice. Refresh our souls again and make us new. Amen.

FOR COURAGE

Dear God, I am afraid. I can see part of the road ahead but not all of it. All kinds of questions buzz around my head. Not that I don't know what needs to be done right now, it's just the not knowing what the outcome will be, how others will react, and what the next steps will have to be.

I ask for your gifts of courage and perseverance. I claim your promise to Joshua long ago always to be with us "withersoever thou goest" and thank you in anticipation that it will be so. Thanks be to God. So be it.

FOR SUCCESS IN SOME CHALLENGING TASK – AN IMPORTANT EXAM, A KEY JOB INTERVIEW OR SOME SIMILAR, STRESS-PRODUCING EVENT

Supreme Intelligence and Creator of the Cosmos, grant me a deep sense of your presence and power in my life now as I prepare for tomorrow. Help me to be at my best and to use thoroughly all my preparation and the abilities you have given to me. I ask for the kind of success that I trust is in accordance with your divine will both for my life and for all those directly affected by it. May whatever happens be to your glory and the greatest common good. Amen.

PRAYERS FROM OTHER SOURCES

One of the readers of my newspaper column, a young Toronto woman, responded to a suggestion I had put out for people to compose their own "set" prayers for daily use. The article in question discussed "The Lord's Prayer" and the headline read: "A Good Place to Start Growing in Prayer."[2] The young woman freely admitted to some "borrowing."

THE SEEKER'S PRAYER

Almighty God, fountain of all goodness, you who are our mother and our father, our friend and the source of all being. Dear One who is closer than our own breathing, may your name be honored and kept sacred – in my life, in my work and in my home, in our nation and in the world, by the way we treat others, and in the way we treat ourselves and our environment. May we heed your teaching and put aside our self-interest to create a just and healing society where all creatures and Mother Earth are honored and treasured.

Give us today the sustenance and spirit to sustain us in our quest. Forgive us when we err, and give us the wisdom and strength to forgive those who cause us pain. Lead me away from self-indulgence as well as the temptation to love myself less than you intend.

May I leave this world a better place because of my journey. Give me strength to rise above my fears, and to take risks so that my gifts of intelligence, caring, vision, humor, and compassion may be shared with others. Help me to rise above my pain so that I may turn my learning there into a gift which benefits the world.

Glory be to you our God and our Creator. I am your servant and your vehicle. Use me to create peace and good will; fill me with your presence. Accept my humble thanks for all you have given me for thine is the kingdom and the glory, for ever and ever. Amen.

A Hindu prayer by one of the most distinguished gurus of this century, the late Gurudev Sivananda of Rishikesh, of India, was kindly sent to me by Swami Gopalanda who helps direct the Yasodhara Ashram, and the Temple of Divine Light on the shores of Lake Kootenay in the southern interior of British Columbia, Canada.

THE UNIVERSAL PRAYER

O adorable Lord of Mercy and Love!
Salutations and prostrations unto Thee.
Thou art Omnipresent, Omnipotent, Omniscient.
Thou art Satchidananda.
Thou art the indweller of all beings.
Grant us an understanding heart,
Equal vision, balanced mind,
Faith, devotion and wisdom.
Grant us inner spiritual strength
To resist temptation and to control the mind.
Free us from egoism, lust, greed, hatred and jealousy.

Fill our hearts with divine virtues.
Let us behold Thee in all these names and forms.
Let us serve Thee in all these names and forms.
Let us ever remember Thee.
Let us ever sing Thy glories.
Let Thy Name be ever on our lips.
Let us abide in Thee for ever and ever.

ON LOVING KINDNESS OR COMPASSION, THE TRUE CORE OF ALL RELIGION AND SPIRITUALITY

The Yasodhara Ashram, with its lovely many-sided, white temple witnessing to the Light in all the major religions of the world, was founded and for many years inspired and directed by a remarkable woman whom I once interviewed during my first days as a journalist in the early 1970s. Swami Radha, as she was known ever since her initiation and blessing by S. Sivananda in Rishkishesh in 1956, was born in Germany in 1911, came to Canada in 1951, and died in 1995. She authored ten books[3] and established a very spiritual form of yoga and meditation with centers in the United States, England, and several places in Canada. To visit her ashram in the mountainous wilds of southern British Columbia today is a remarkable experience. My wife and I did so recently (the last part of the journey is by car ferry and seems like going to one of Earth's last frontiers!) and we were particularly impressed by *The Sutra on Loving Kindness* frequently used at the evening *Satsang*, or service, in the temple. As we attended a service the first evening and as the prayer was being said in unison, the lake lay shimmering like hammered gold below and the snow-capped mountain crests gleamed brightly against a still, gold and purple sky to the west. In the note accompanying an official copy of the Sutra (in Hindu tradition, a Sutra is a holy book or series of sacred verses), S. Gopalanda said this prayer always opened Satsang each evening at Sivananda Ashram in Rishkishesh when S. Radha was there and so it became one of her favorites. It is lengthy but very powerful and searching in its depth and scope. It is reproduced here by permission.

May I be free from greed, hate, and delusion.
May I be full of self-sacrifice, love, and understanding.

I charge my heart, that is now temporarily pure, with thoughts of
Loving Kindness.
I charge every cell of my being with thoughts of Loving Kindness.
I build a healthy, happy aura of Loving Kindness around me,
that no wicked thought or evil intention can penetrate.
Now I am protected.

I now send forth thoughts of Loving Kindness
to all beings and creatures
to everything animate and inanimate
to everything that has taken rise in consciousness
and to everything still in its causal state.

I send forth these thoughts around me
around my dwelling
around my district
around the continent
around the world.
Loving Kindness to all, Loving Kindness to all.
Around the universe, Loving Kindness to all.
Around the cosmos, Loving Kindness, Loving Kindness to all.

Loving Kindness to all who dwell above and
Loving Kindness to those who dwell below.

May all beings and creatures
And everything animate and inanimate
And everything that has reached Consciousness
And everything still in its causal state,
May all be happily minded.
May none hurt each other in anger and ill will.
May their minds be wholesome.
May all have sufficient for their needs.
May all be fortunate enough to encounter the Dharma [The Way].

Humbly I accept the loving thoughts of everyone in return.
None excluded.

And now I share the benefit of this meditation with everyone.

There can be no doubt whatever that daily praying such a prayer
can be a transforming experience for an individual. Imagine,
then, the vast, seismic, spiritual and social effects of whole communities and eventually entire peoples joining regularly in this
kind of intention and intercession. Even if the results were completely explained by sceptics or naysayers in terms of autosuggestion or self-hypnosis, they would, I believe, amaze us. Of
course, I personally believe much more would be going on than
mere self-hypnosis or autosuggestion. This kind of widely shared
openness and all-embracing compassion would resonate in tune
with the way God has made the whole universe to vibrate and
"hang together." Peace, harmony, and social justice would roll

down "like an ever-flowing stream," to borrow a phrase from the prophet Amos (5:24), and as never before in history.

A PRAYER AFFIRMATION OF THE POWER AND PRESCENCE OF THE DIVINE LIGHT

Swami Radha, who was so much more aware than most, of the difficulties we have when speaking or imaging about the Ultimate Reality we call God, found that what worked best for her was the image and metaphor of Supreme Light. It is, of course, one way of seeing and describing God that is common to most religions. As the Latin motto of Oxford University boldly states: *Deus illuminatio mea.* The Lord is my Light (from Psalm 27:1). But, for her, it became the center and source of her whole spirituality. Here, by special permission, is her *Invocation to the Divine Light* which became her lifelong often-repeated prayer or mantra.

> *I am created by Divine Light.*
> *I am sustained by Divine Light.*
> *I am protected by Divine Light.*
> *I am surrounded by Divine Light.*
> *I am ever growing into Divine Light.*[4]

Some of these prayers may well not be appropriate for you. Others will seem right on target. So, once more, let me encourage you to change any or all of them and adapt them more nearly to your own feelings, needs and ways. The important thing is eventually to get some vital, simple prayers you can imagine yourself using over a reasonably long period of time. They will prove a great resource and a support to the totally spontaneous "arrow prayers" you will increasingly find yourself using as you make the habit of "praying without ceasing" your own.

A PROJECT

1. Take any prayer from the above and write it out in the way that makes best sense to you. You may find yourself making several drafts before arriving at the one you like, the one you can actually see yourself praying. Once you have polished and honed it, make a proper copy, preferably on a typewriter or computer, and keep it nearby for daily use.

2. Look at my list of topics one more time. If this were your sample list, what other topics would have been included? Try writing brief prayers of your own on those themes. Which of mine would you have left out?

VIII

PRAYERS OF PRAISE

God is our refuge and strength,
a very present help in trouble.
Therefore we will not fear...
Psalm 46:1–2a

————

For mortals it is impossible,
but for God all things are possible.
Matthew 19:26

————

Blessed be the Lord,
for he has wondrously shown his steadfast love to me
when I was beset as a city under seige.
Psalm 31:21

One of the most significant, simple, and obvious points which I deliberately repeat several times in this book is that prayer is such a many-splendored thing. Too many of us are still tightly locked into a one-dimensional model. Prayer, as a conversation not with some abstract "divine force" or energy but with a personal God, can have all the changing modes and "voices" of intimate conversation with a lover or a best friend.[1] The popular version of prayer is often really a special sort of childish "gimme, gimme" (the technical, theological name for this type is "prayers of petition" or "supplication"), or else something we inevitably associate with clergy and with formal occasions in a church, synagogue or temple. The reality of prayer, however, is kaleidoscopic in range, style or format. Most certainly it is not something to be left almost completely to ministers or other ecclesiastical persons!

I have already mentioned what are often called prayers of affirmation. In these, instead of asking for specific things or making other requests, one simply affirms – either silently or aloud – some basic, spiritual truths. As, for example, in the often-repeated Muslim affirmation: "God is great." When this is done repeatedly, the statement then becomes, however we may think of it ourselves, a sort of personal mantra for meditation. This can be particularly effective when it's combined with an act of visualization at the same time. For example, if it is a verse or line from some well-loved sacred scripture, from a hymn, a poem or a song, it's possible to use one's imagination simultaneously to imagine whatever is being said actually coming true. If you don't know what to pray for a friend who is ill, you can always affirm that God is light while you imagine your friend surrounded, bathed, and protected by dazzling light – a light even beyond the brightness of the sun, a light which is pure love. You can visualize your friend being raised up and held by you in the light as you ask for their wholeness to be restored.

In Chapter 2, I cited Dr. Dean Ornish, author of *Reversing Heart Disease*. Ornish recommends that those who suffer coronary artery disease spend about 10 minutes daily visualizing a mystical light, or any other imagery that appeals, which floods the heart and then the whole body, eventually spreading out to other people. Patients are encouraged to "see" this light healing the "lesions" or the blockages in their heart arteries and opening them to a renewed flow of blood. It works for a very high percentage of those who stick with the regimen.

Susan and I attended one of Ornish's week-long retreats in Berkeley, California, in the spring of 1997. Others attending – nearly all of them men – had undergone bypasses or angioplasties, or had suffered from angina so painful they could barely shave or walk across the street a few years ago. It was quite inspiring to hear these people describe how they were now free of all pain and most medications. One 82-year-old named Werner seemed amazingly full of energy and vitality. He told everyone of his recovery and of how he had never felt so good in 20 years since his first heart attack.

If you are suffering from fear and anxiety, it can help enormously to affirm and to visualize that God's strength and powerful presence are with you right at this moment, and always. It can help even more if you take some sacred symbol or persona (light, Jesus, Krishna, Buddha) for this great source of calmness and courage, and envision this presence with, beside, or within you. The Hebrew Psalms, as we have seen, are extraordinarily rich in this kind of resource. So too are the New Testament and, of course, the Qur'an and many other sacred texts from other religions. For example, for Christians, the words of 2 Timothy 1:7

– "For God hath not given us the spirit of fear; but of power, and of love, and of a sound mind" – lend themselves directly to use as a mantra with their bold affirmation of hope. We should choose our own favorites from these at some time of serenity in order to have them ready at hand when panic, discouragement or doubts assail.

There are many books around now on various techniques for therapeutic visualization so there's little reason to repeat them here. But certainly most of us could do with some regular stretching of our imagination when it comes to spiritual matters. One of the most stirring of all the great stories in the Hebrew Bible (rather pejoratively called "The Old Testament" by Christians and others) always comes to my mind in this regard. It is found in the Second Book of Kings, at a point when the king of Syria is seeking to find and kill the prophet Elisha (2 Kings 6:15ff). On the run, trying to elude the angry monarch, Elisha had taken refuge in a small town in the hill country called Dothan. Early one morning, his young attendant went for a walk on top of the walls of the city and discovered that the Syrians had come stealthily during the night and were now camped and surrounding the place. He ran back to his master and told him the dire situation they were now in. "Alas, master! What shall we do?" he cries out.

Elisha calmly tells the young man not to be afraid: "For there are more with us than there are with them." The youth looks about and doesn't have the slightest idea as to where these unknown, alleged allies and helpers are to be found. Then Elisha prays, "O Lord, please open his eyes that he may see." So, the text says, God opened the eyes of the servant, "and he saw; the mountain was full of horses and chariots of fire all around Elisha." Both of them escaped to safety.

Through learning to practice visualization, we too can learn to "see" with imagination and with the eyes of faith that there are energies and forces on our side we had never imagined before. This is not a matter of indulging our fancies or living in a never-neverland. It's a training of our hearts and minds to claim what is already ours as children of God, while at the same time working to bring it about. As with any great human endeavor, thoughts and imagery come into being before the reality is achieved – before the plan is ever executed, the book written, or the symphony composed. First the mind "sees," and then the universe, by the grace of God and with our help, brings it to birth.

What I chiefly want to consider in this chapter, however, is not so much affirmation praying, with visualization, but another form of nonpetitionary prayer altogether: the prayer of praise, thanksgiving and worship.

Sceptics and others who object to prayer have a serious point to make at this juncture. It is one which used to bother me too as an undergraduate years ago. In a nutshell, the problem is this: why should God or the Source of all Being desire our praise and worship through prayers or in any other way? Isn't it a form of serious psychopathology to want and need to be told how great and good one is when one is only being true to one's nature in any case? Isn't it enough for God to be God, without continuously wanting to be, as it were, flattered because of it?

The answer here, I believe, is similar to that already given in the case of those who stumble over the question, "Why pray when God already knows all you're going to say anyway?" What finally ended my own unease and uncertainty on this point was the argument that of course God does not need either our most elaborate worship or our most exalted, ardent praise. We alone are the ones with the need to adore and give thanks. There are times when you feel as though you would burst if there was nobody (Nobody!) there to thank. I think the hardest part of being an agnostic or an atheist must be feeling full of praise and thanksgiving for any one of life's amazing miracles and gifts – like a snow-topped mountain with the sunset all around it, a glorious fall day in the countryside, a tiny infant's first smile, or the experience of being wildly in love – and yet having no Source or God to thank. Apart, that is, from that remorseless, pseudodeity called random chance or sheer luck.

But our need for worship and praise goes deeper than this. Human beings have an insatiable yearning and need to give worth, ultimate worth (worship means worth-ship) to something or Someone beyond ourselves. Get rid of the Creator God and people instantly worship a host of other things, some quite dangerous, others utterly superficial or even bizarre. For example, they will worship some form of the political state, professional sports, sexual pleasure, or celebrity status. Other people might idolize a range of other sources of putative bliss, control, or ostentation: their homes and automobiles; their own bodies; television, electronic gadgets, or other pieces of techno-wizardry; the latest styles in clothing; gourmet food; or money itself. The list of idols or alternatives to God in Western culture at this moment would make the most primitive idolater of ancient times seem like a mere novice, a fumbling amateur. The new idolatries of consumerism, pushed and aided by the worldwide communication web and other media tools, are on a far vaster scale than anything this Earth has ever previously witnessed. These false gods, unfortunately, demand sacrifices. The cost to the unwitting worshippers, though it may seem hidden at times, is ultimately very high – the loss of our true humanity and irreparable damage to Earth and its wonders.

We need to worship and serve a Supreme Being, some personal, communicating form of Ultimacy. We were made or "wired" by God for that and prayer is one of the major ways in which this adoration and praise can be expressed freely, joyfully, and in a myriad of different ways. It can be done through words, but also, as the study of aboriginal spirituality and other ancient religious rites amply illustrates, through dancing, mime, or other art forms. Body positions and movements – whether more elaborate, as in certain forms of yoga; or quite simple, as in the rocking motion of Jews praying at the "Wailing Wall" in Jerusalem; whether the raised hands of Pentecostals or Charismatic Christians; or the kneeling of Anglicans, Roman Catholics, Lutherans, and others; whether the seemingly frenetic spinning of the "whirling dervish" in mystical Islam; or the more familiar five-times-a-day prostrations of the world's nearly one billion Muslims – are an important nonverbal part of praying as well. One prays with the body as well as with the soul.

SINGING AND CHANTING

Singing and, in particular, chanting, can be verbal or nonverbal too. No single aspect of the religious and spiritual life of our entire species is more universally practiced than chanting. There are a number of reasons for this. Before the modern era and the advent of the printing press, the best way to keep and pass on a tradition, a spiritual formation, or various sacred texts was to recite them in a chanted rhythm and tune. In all the ages without sound amplification, it was also the best method for ensuring that everyone could hear the liturgy or worship. In addition, chanting best lent itself to the repetition of sacred mantras made up of either especially sacred words or nonverbal sounds. There is, however, more to chanting than any of this suggests.

Recently, scientists studying the therapeutic effects of sound on human health have discovered that certain repeated and hummed or sung syllables definitely have a benign influence on our whole body-mind-spirit connection. Significantly, recent studies of the extent of depression suffered by monks and sisters in monasteries and nunneries of the Roman Catholic Church in Europe, for example, have shown that there was a marked correlation between an increasing rate of mood disorders and the giving up of chanting by many such communities in the wake of Vatican II (1962–65). When and where the practice of chanting was resumed, the incidence of depression dropped significantly. There is a deep and urgent human need that is being met in the sudden and amazing popularity today of recordings of Gregorian chanting. Singing and listening to singing makes us feel good. It's not "just psychological" either, whatever that expression really means. It has a strong physiological basis as recent scientific research has also shown. The act of intoning, chanting, or singing, massages or stimulates important glands and/or organs.

Once you begin to compare the preferred sounds employed by the devotees of the various religions, from aboriginal to Buddhist, from Islamic to Hindu, you will be astounded at their similarity. I have suggested Amen or Shalom as possible mantras for meditation. Notice how both have an "ah" sound as well as an Aum or Om. Both of these are believed to be healing sounds as well as reverential. In the case of the latter, it's because it repeats aspects of the primal vibration, the "word," by which Hindus believe the world was made. It is not an accident that the Hebrew word of praise, hallelujah or alleluia, is resonant with ah sounds. Notice too that the Muslim name for God, Allah, also features two ahs; the Hebrew name for God, Yahweh has both an ah and an "eh" (pronounced *ay* as in *say*) which is also common in ancient chants. There are many other vowels or diphthongs one could cite; for example, "ung" or "oong" can be hummed or chanted with an emphasis on causing the roof of one's mouth to vibrate. This is believed, among other things, to vibrate and energize the pineal gland, in the center of one's skull and one of the master glands ruling over bodily health.[2]

True, chanting has been growing in popularity in the West ever since the 1960s. But to chant, either some favorite psalm or hymn, or, to my own surprise, simply a series of primal, sacred sounds such as I have listed – just repeating one for a few minutes and then changing to another – is a new and very powerful form of praise which I have recently rediscovered for myself. Whether it is just autosuggestion or not I cannot yet state for certain; but I believe it has made a real difference in my personal prayer life and in my health. Buddhist monks in the East are encouraged to do their chanting by a river so that nobody can hear them. I do it only on the most solitary parts of my daily walks. Use your own judgment on how to do it without disturbing others or without being thought to have "flipped" completely this time. Try it and experiment for yourself.

PRAYER AS ACTION

One of prayer's most effective, nonverbal expressions, though, is in some form of positive action: in one's work done well, in deeds of kindness and compassion, in greater commitment to social justice. Praise or worship that is solely made up of rites, songs, affirmations, or other verbalizing, and that stops there, is in the end vain and false. The true test of the integrity of any worship, whether private or public, is what it leads to (or doesn't) in terms of changed lives for the worshippers, and changed conditions for the poor, the oppressed, and the abandoned. How often in the Hebrew Bible do the prophets make the point that God "hates" the would-be noise and even the smell of solemn assemblies when they are not accompanied by genuine concern and a deliberate working for justice for all![3]

The late George MacLeod (Baron MacLeod of Fiunary), founder of the restored Iona Community just off the west coast of Scotland, once preached a sermon in which he told of a church in England which had a stained glass window based on the nativity story and carrying the text in upper case, "GLORY TO GOD IN THE HIGHEST AND ON EARTH PEACE, GOODWILL AMONG MEN." However, some mischievous youngster had flung a stone at the window and thus accidentally erased the E from HIGHEST. The result looked like: GLORY TO GOD IN THE HIGH ST AND ON EARTH... MacLeod went on to say, aptly, that unless worship inside a church or temple leads to God's glory (his/her worship) out in the High St. (North Americans would say, on "Main Street") of every town and city, it is a bogus kind of praise. "Praising God on High St." could have formed a fitting motto of the whole approach MacLeod himself used as he tried to apply the Christian gospel in practical ways to modern, urbanized living in Scotland and beyond.

As suggested before, you can pray the Psalms, most of them at any rate, to assist you in your private prayers of praise. Here again, it's good to have one or two lines that are memorized and then can be called to mind whenever there's a special reason for being thankful. For example, I particularly like, and use myself, the opening lines of Psalm 103.

Bless the Lord, O my soul.
and all that is within me,
bless God's holy name.

Bless the Lord, O my soul,
and do not forget all God's benefits –
who forgives all your iniquity [sin]
who heals all your diseases,
who redeems your life from the pit,
who crowns you with
steadfast love and mercy,
who satisfies you with good
as long as you live,
so that your youth is
renewed like the eagle's.

(An Inclusive Language Lectionary)

Those of different faiths can readily find fitting passages or lines in their own Qur'an, Bhagavad-Gita, the Sikhs' Adi Granth, or in other similar major religious texts. Jews, in addition to the Hebrew Bible, for example, are naturally very familiar with the words from The Kaddish, the traditional prayer of mourning. It begins,

Let us magnify and let us sanctify the great name of God in the
world which he created... May the greatness of his being be blessed
from eternity to eternity. Let us bless and let us extol, let us tell
aloud, and let us raise aloft, let us set on high and let us honor, let
us exalt and let us praise the Holy One – Blessed be He! – though
he is far above any blessing or song, and honor or any consolation
that can be spoken of in this world.

For Muslims, there are many fine examples also, particularly the opening words of their revered Qu'ran.

> *In the name of God, the merciful Lord of mercy.*
> *Praise be to God, the Lord of all being,*
> *the merciful Lord of mercy,*
> *master of the day of judgment.*
> *You alone we serve: to you alone we come for aid...*
>
> Surah 1: The Opener

And here is a Shinto prayer from Japan, a prayer of thanks and praise at evening.

> *I reverently speak in the presence of the Great Parent God;*
> *I give thee grateful thanks that thou hast enabled me to live this day,*
> *the whole day, in obedience to the excellent spirit of thy ways.*

What has been most helpful to me in trying to be as faithful as possible in making and praying daily prayers of praise, thanksgiving and worship (though I confess I too sometimes forget) is the awareness of how much this strengthens a positive, faith-full outlook on current problems, and on those certain to come in the future. It cannot be stressed too frequently that the act of "counting one's blessings," as the old evangelistic hymn puts it, has a powerful, therapeutic message: what God has done before, God can do again. As we are surprised by "what the Lord has done" in our lives in the past, we are encouraged and enriched now and as we look ahead. "Thank you" is one of the most all-encompassing, essential prayers of them all. Of all the prayers in the 1962 *Anglican Book of Common Prayer*, the one I admire the most is the General Thanksgiving. It begins as follows: "Almighty God, Father of all mercies, We thine unworthy servants do give thee most humble and hearty thanks for all thy goodness and loving kindness to us and to all [people]..."[4]

A PROJECT

List the first five things which come to mind when you consider the following question: "What am I most thankful to God for at this exact moment in my life?" Now, taking these five, compose a brief, simple prayer in which you tell God what they are and why it is you feel particularly grateful for them right now. End it with an honest, heartfelt sentence or two of thanks and praise. This makes a helpful, deeply satisfying way to begin or end the day no matter what else is crowding the forefront of your mind.

IX

KEEPING A
PRAYER DIARY

Do not worry about anything,
but in everything by prayer and supplication with thanksgiving
let your requests be made known to God.
The Apostle Paul, Letter to the Philippians, 4:6

———

O you who answer prayer!
To you all flesh shall come.

Psalm 65:2

———

Watch [stay awake] and pray...
the spirit indeed is willing but the flesh is weak.

Jesus in Gethsemane, Matthew 26:41

Many people today keep a spiritual diary in which they record their thoughts, struggles, special inspirations and insights, moments of growth as well as times of failure or "dryness." I suggest that if you don't do this – even if you do – you might also want to consider a prayer diary. Nothing is a truer record of your inner life than a listing, however brief, of the chief matters which daily occupy your meditations and praying. Rereading such a diary from time to time can act as a shaper of your prayers in the future and as a history of your ongoing odyssey towards and in God. Of course, nothing about it is obligatory. You can grow steadily in prayer without it. But keeping one for a while now has made me realize afresh what an independent, strong source of inspiration and renewal it can be in one's life. Among other things, it helps keep me from growing stale or formal in my prayers. In particular, the phenomenon of "answered prayer" can be specifically documented over time. If you are experimenting with prayer in a real way for the first time, it gives you a sort of laboratory record, a kindling of fresh faith and of an even more honest sense of wonder and praise.

Here's a brief sampling (expanded, however, from a kind of shorthand or code style I use in order to save time) from my own prayer journal during some of the time in 1997 that I spent in writing this book.

MAY 11

Susan and I went to morning worship today at an historic Quaker Meeting House, on the outskirts of Newmarket, about a 15-minute drive from our home. We'd been there before because of our love of the silence and the simple beauty of the clapboard building, the huge, gnarled trees guarding the door, and the quiet country cemetery nearby. In spite of one of the main roads in

Canada (Yonge Street) passing the gates and an explosion of new homes, malls and other developments all around, it remains an amazingly calm oasis of peace. In Quaker worship, there is no minister or priest and no formal order of service. At the meeting house I'm describing, you sit facing others on stiff, wooden benches around the four sides of the square space which is the area for the Meeting. All that is in the room by way of ornament – and indeed its true nature is functional and not esthetic – is an old woodstove right in the middle of everything. There is no hymn-singing, no formal praying, and no sermon or formal offering. Worshippers sit in utter silence, meditating on the Inner Light, seeking guidance and illumination, for the entire hour. Silence is only broken when someone (anyone) gets up and shares very briefly some insight or "message" from their inner contemplation. Occasionally, you can go the full hour without a word being spoken. Announcements are made once the "service" has ended.

As we took our place, it was a glorious morning with brilliant sunshine pouring in the dust-stained windows and songbirds trilling their hearts out beyond the walls. Thrilled with the evident signs of spring – at last! This spring has been much more reluctant than most, even for Ontario. The opening lines of Psalm 27 began to resonate at my core.

> *The Lord is my light and my*
> *salvation;*
> *whom shall I fear?*
> *the Lord is the refuge of my life,*
> *of whom shall I be afraid?*
> Verses 1ff

As we sat in the deep quiet and meditated further, I finally felt moved to share a meditation or prayer, ignited by the psalm, with the few others there. There was no written text, but this is it as close as I can remember it:

"The Lord is our light and our final wholeness" – which is what salvation really means. This morning, we all are aware of the spring sunshine. We, together with the whole sacred community of Earth's living things, rejoice in it. After the long winter, there's a primitive longing, in spite of warnings about various dangers from radiation, to bathe ourselves in that sunlight. We thank God for the sun, the source of life for this planet and not unreasonably regarded in the past by many peoples in many places as itself a god.

But we know the psalmist is not talking about this kind of light. For him, as for us, there is a Light beyond all physical light, the light that "gives light to every person as it comes into the world," the light which in almost all of the great religions can be found as the ultimate image or symbol of the living God. This morning, we are seeking to bathe our inner selves in that Light. My prayer is that this may be so for me and for us all. And so, healed and with a fresh vision of that Light, may we go forth from here renewed within and with a fresh resolve to be channels of the Light in all we do, not just for our own sakes but for those suffering the darkness of injustice or the bite of pain in a bleeding world. Amen, so be it.

In retrospect, it sounds perhaps a little preachy, but it wasn't intended to be.

MAY 12

This morning's newspaper had an overwhelmingly sad story from a remote mountain oasis village called Ardakul, in Iran. The headline said, "God, God, why are you punishing us?" and was a quote from Mohammad Aijan, a villager who at one moment was kissing his nine-year-old daughter on both cheeks before she raced down the road to school and scarcely ten minutes later found himself reeling under the shock of news that a most terrible disaster had struck. Later, after ten hours of frantic digging and searching, he lifted his little girl's crushed body from the ruins of the collapsed schoolhouse. It had been turned into a pile of jagged slabs of concrete and twisted steel by a sudden and devastating earthquake. The tragic story said that Aijan's daughter, Mahbubeh, was one of 110 girls killed at the school by the quake which measured over 7 on the Richter scale.

More than 500 of the 1600 residents of the village were killed in a twinkling of an eye and, in the neighboring village of Zohan, at least 60 pupils, also Muslims, were killed in the very act of saying their midday prayers. The entire area for kilometers around, wherever there were buildings of any kind, was in ruins. Those who escaped were mainly men out at work in the fields or guarding their flocks and herds.

(A later note: The following day, there were much fuller reports putting the number of deaths caused by the earthquake at well over 1,600.)

What added to the impact of this story on me – and admittedly it pales by comparison with many other terrible disasters which are reported by the media with soul-numbing frequency these days – was that on the previous evening I had been to a cinema to see a very sensitive and moving award-winning Iranian film entitled *Gabbeh*. The kind of terrain and people, the pastoral kind of lifestyle so lovingly and tenderly caressed by the camera in *Gabbeh* were precisely the same as those of the Ardakul region of Iran. The lives and faces of the old, the adult men and women and the little children there which had been so eloquently portrayed by the movie – all but identical with those who were the chief victims of the quake – were very much in my mind as I read the accounts of the current tragedy.

What to pray? No words of mine or from anybody else could ever be adequate. Yet, apart from responding to appeals for aid by the relevant agencies, what other way is there to deal with such a terrible loss? Though far away and with a culture so strikingly different in many ways from ours, nevertheless these people are much more like us than they are dissimilar. They feel pain and grief – and anger at God – as deeply as any of us would in such a plight. They are our brothers and sisters, our fathers and mothers, our grandparents, and our children, since we share a single origin and are "made of one blood to dwell upon the Earth."

I prayed along these lines: "God of all mercy, I don't even begin to comprehend this tragedy, this awful event. Comfort those who have been bereaved, especially those who have had their little ones taken from them. Help and strengthen them as they bear their grief and go about the giant task of trying to rebuild their lives. I ask particularly for your blessing and guidance for all who right now are trying to supply medical aid, shelter and food for the survivors at Ardakul, at Zohan, and elsewhere. Move our hearts with compassion and a willingness to support this aid effort wherever and to whatever extent we can, both by our prayers and by our giving." (For an in-depth discussion of the problem of innocent suffering, please see Chapter 4, "The Power of Evil," in my book *Would You Believe? Finding God Without Losing Your Mind*.)

MAY 15

I spent about four hours working at my computer today and wrote several pages for my book. However, when I had finished, I somehow made a huge error when it came to "saving" or keeping this part of a new chapter. Somehow I managed to get the process backwards and I imposed the text as it was *before* I began writing this morning from the hard drive onto the disk. The new material was effectively erased, gone, kaput. I couldn't believe I had done it and was at first certain that if I searched long enough the lost section would turn up. But after about 30 increasingly anxious and hectic minutes, I was forced to give up in total frustration. Few things are as dismaying and irritating as losing something you have labored hard and at length to create. The experts say that this kind of accident is impossible. Yet it happens. I felt depressed and empty for the rest of the day. I knew I would have to start all over again tomorrow, but for a time I had my enthusiasm dampened to say the least.

I finally realized I needed to pray about it. Quite boldly, I shared my feelings of chagrin at my own carelessness, my anger at the situation, and my temporary loss of confidence. I asked for patience and the grace to remember enough of what I had written to provide a framework for the repeat performance tomorrow. Surprisingly, to me at any rate, the feelings of heaviness and disappointment left almost instantly. I forgave myself and resolved to be a lot smarter in the future when it comes to turning my machine off at the end of a day's work.

A later note: While I never got back the original missing paragraphs, by the following morning I felt not only ready but eager to attempt writing the pages anew. They turned out, I believe, to be significantly better than the first version!

MAY 18

This weekend, the Victoria Day long weekend in Canada, Susan and I drove up to the fishing, scuba diving and tourist center of Tobermory, Ontario, right up on the tip of the Bruce Peninsula, which thrusts itself out into Georgian Bay. My brother, who is a family physician and diving specialist, lives there with his family in a house built right on the cliffs facing out over the Bay, towards Manitoulin Island. My mother lives not far away in a seniors' residence overlooking the picturesque harbor.

Tonight, Susan and I made dinner for a family crowd at my brother's place and, of course, my mum was there. Luckily, she has enjoyed fairly vigorous health throughout her senior years and has been quite independent. She still has a valid driver's license. Lately, however, she has become very unsteady on her feet and has suffered a series of bad falls in spite of using a cane. We had dinner and eventually the large dining-kitchen area was empty except for my mother, seated at the far end of a long dining table, and myself washing up a couple of utensils at an "island" some distance away. Suddenly, out of the corner of my eye, I saw her coming along, without her cane, but steadying herself with one hand on the table. Before I could get there she had launched into the space between the table and the center spot where I was working. She failed to make contact as she reached out for the edge of the counter where I was and a sudden look of fear came over her face. I realized two things at once: she was about to fall on the hardwood floor and there was no way I could get there soon enough to stop it. She made an effort to right herself, slipped badly, and crashed down on her side and back, simultaneously cracking her head backwards into an open cabinet below. I said a lot of "arrow prayers" as I dashed around to her and as people began running to the kitchen from all parts of the house. We felt devastated and sick at heart as we waited for an ambulance to arrive.

A later note: She spent a week in hospital – the lump on the back of her head was almost the size of an orange – but remarkably had done no really serious damage to any of her major bones. With the aid of a walker she was soon able to get around once again. We prayed a lot around this event; about her recovery, certainly, being careful to give thanks for no broken hips or neck vertebrae, but also about wisdom for a proper approach to her future care and whether or not this might be the time for her independent lifestyle to come to a close. These decisions have yet to be made as I write.[1]

Incidentally, within the same ten-day period that included my mum's fall, hospitalization and brief rehabilitation, Susan's mother and dad, who live in different wings of a seniors' residence and nursing home in downtown Toronto were both whisked to hospital emergency units. (Sue's mother had a severe stroke during heart surgery over 12 years ago and her father, who has made a very fine recovery, suffered a heart attack during kidney surgery a couple of years later.) Both are better now, thankfully, but between all of that and at least two other family crises I won't go into here, we felt we'd had another little taste of "where the rubber meets the road." This is not to complain at all. We've been very fortunate. These are the kind of experiences that transform writing about prayer into a practical project and not one of merely airy-fairy theorizing.

JUNE 6

If it is true that "in God we live and move and have our being,"
as Paul says in Acts, then nothing which concerns our lives is
too small, or unimportant in the overall scheme of things. Nothing about us is alien to God's compassion and care. I know people
who refuse to "bring everything to God in prayer," as the Bible
– and Joseph Scriven in his well-known hymn *What a Friend We
Have in Jesus* – exhorts us to do, because they believe they need
to somehow hoard a store of God's good will against the day
when a major crisis hits and the need will be terribly urgent.
But it's not a case of drawing upon a limited and very specific
power source. God cares about all of our life or about none of it.
There are no limits to the ocean of energy available to us. That's
why those who believe in prayer and have found it to work,
hold to the first option.

Today was an example of this. It had to do with a very
common experience, that of losing something small but of
great importance – not necessarily in others' eyes but from our
own perspective. I'm far from proud of it, but I have always
had a tendency to misplace or lose things such as car keys,
other keys, and other small but similarly intrinsic parts of what
Susan calls "Tom's kit." When I had a parish to care for, the
church secretary would regularly see me searching my pockets
or office for something and quip: "Are you still looking for
those keys?" During my pipe-smoking years I seemed to spend
a lot of the time looking for matches, a pipe, my tobacco – or
all three.

What happened today was, to me, remarkable. I have been
missing a unique set of keys for my car, our mailbox and the
house, for about a month. When I first lost them, I became quite
upset with myself for my carelessness. I was certain they weren't

"lost"; it was just that I couldn't remember where I had put them. I went around searching the house, my clothes, the car and every other imaginable hiding place until I felt it would drive me to total distraction. So I stopped searching, prayed about them – with a sinking feeling of futility – and borrowed Susan's keys instead.

Today, after driving Susan to the bus for her commute to business in downtown Toronto, I decided to take the day off and go fishing for the first time in quite a while. I packed all my gear hastily and, after a two-hour drive north, found myself on one of the wildest, choicest runs of rapids in southern Ontario. I used to fish there for rainbow trout some years ago – with considerable success – but for one reason or another it seemed my life had simply been too busy or, when I did go to a river or lake, that I had fished elsewhere. It was a completely glorious day. Because of the late spring, everything was in bloom along the river. The clear, clean water roared in white foam over a series of falls and then slid in smooth, lavish currents over the rock-strewn, sun-dappled riverbed. After the chute of white water, the stream then widened into a long, narrow lake with a dam at the end.

Nothing happened at first. But before too long, I caught one good-sized trout, then a second somewhat smaller. I missed two more and then lost a favorite lure. I was wearing an old, tattered fishing vest I hadn't had on except for the one other time I had been trout fishing this year. As I reached into one of the pockets for another spinner lure, I felt something quite unlike an artificial bait. To my amazement, it was my lost key-fob with all the keys intact! I haven't the slightest idea of how they came to be there. At once I made a brief, quite informal yet intensely sincere prayer of thanks – for the day, for the chance to be fishing again, but above all for "accidentally" recovering my loss. I also resolved to be more careful, more truly mindful of such essential, though small, things in the future. Susan was more than relieved to see her own borrowed set back in her own hands again!

JUNE 10

From time to time I find I make commitments to speak at or to lead conferences that lie a year or two in the future. They seem so far away that it's an easy step to assume the responsibility without a care in the world. Suddenly, however, a day comes when they seem to loom out of nowhere on one's calendar. Since lots of other things, including fresh media and other commitments, have come up in the meanwhile, I find I can then have a tendency to feel acute discomfort, even fear bordering on panic. That's certainly the case at the moment as it has finally sunk in that I have two major events coming up in the interior of British Columbia in the next few weeks. One, at Naramata, the United Church of Canada's adult education center near Penticton, on beautiful Lake Okanagan, consists of giving the keynote lecture and several seminars on spiritual healing over a four-day period. The other, at Sorrento, the Anglican Church of Canada's similar center on Lake Shuswap, near Salmon Arm, involves eight lectures during a week spent considering the theme "Communicating the Good News Today."

In my prayers this morning, and later on as well, I admitted my fears and unexpected apprehensions for these two events. I asked for strength to carry them out and, most important, made a specific commitment to devote the next few days to solid preparation for both. There's nothing like actually being ready,

having faced the discipline and hard work required, to help re-
move irrational doubts and anxieties about any project. I know
I'll still have "performance anxiety" when the occasion finally
presents itself. But that's different from the original panic – and,
like most public speaking or performance of any kind, a slight
tingling in one's stomach can help give an edge. It certainly
keeps one from complacency!

A later note: The two events turned out extremely well. Susan
and I met dozens of wonderful people who were truly concerned about their fellow human beings and the healing both of
the individual and the planet. The scenery at both ends of the
Okanagan Valley was inspiring and soothing to the spirit. With
so many vineyards and orchards between the higher slopes of
the mountains and the sparkling waters of the winding lake below, one was reminded of such European countries as Austria
and Switzerland. In spite of my previous fears and even some
minor panic, I fully enjoyed giving the various talks and they
were very well received. We learned so much from the other
speakers and helpers; we came home, after the second affair,
very glad after all to have agreed to be part of both conferences.
We had a keen sense that God had meant us to be there and are
still most grateful for this experience of answered prayer.

JULY 7

While reading some of the material we picked up at the Yasodhara
Ashram on Kootenay Lake, British Columbia, a couple of weeks
ago, I came across the following prayer suggestion from its founder
and guru, Swami Radha. It had been written some years earlier.

"Pray daily to be shown the blocks that still keep you from
the Divine."

It's such a straightforward, simple petition, yet it struck me as one of the most helpful, potentially powerful recommendations I had read in some time. I have resolved to make frequent use of it because becoming more spiritual is mainly about becoming more conscious of everything within as well as beyond our immediate concerns. To be more conscious of the blocks between ourselves and God is to know what needs the most work as we seek to make progress. I ask God to show me ever more clearly the things blocking the inflow and outflow of the Light in my life.

JULY 20

In my walking meditation this morning the muse or the Spirit within seemed particularly present and "speaking" to me. The truth of what Susan had been saying to me for some time seemed to be the chief "message." I had been wondering about whether or not I was meant to pick up my syndicated column again after my current leave of absence from February 15, 1997 to January 1, 1998. Also, what to do about the increasing spate of invitations to speak at or to lead lecture series, seniors' weekends, and so on. Susan's view was that I should cut down rather than increase the speaking engagements. She reasoned that I could reach more people in a lasting way by concentrating more on writing books and on creating or sharing in more TV programs such as the *Life After Death* series or *The Uncommon Touch*, a six-part series on spiritual healing to be aired in the near future. In any case, the Light within today seemed strongly to confirm her own leading. So I am learning to say "no" even though I find it hard at times.

JULY 23

Susan and I have been thinking and praying for some time now about the next phase of our lives and how to make best use of the time allotted to us; questions involving what further work to do, what travel and other leisure activities to pursue, even where to live. We have prayed hard and long – prayers with suction! – but the only answer coming through so far has been, "Keep on waiting upon God." Imagine my surprise and joy, then, when, as I walked my regular five miles this morning, the ideas began pouring in. I had a sort of brilliant, illuminated eureka experience in which a particular path and approach was outlined within my brain/heart. It needs testing, analysis, further discussion with Susan and further guidance. But we have a strong conviction that what I received is more than simple intuition or sudden "brainwave." It seems like a fulfillment of the prophet's promise that they who wait in patience upon the Lord shall renew their strength and catch a new vision.

––––––––––

There is so much else, failures and disappointments as well as great encouragements and successes to peruse as I look backwards through the diary. But, by now, the concept and practice are clear enough. Keeping a prayer diary is well worth the trouble and time it takes because it is so easy to lose sight of any overall pattern in one's prayer life without it. You so easily forget or overlook the way in which prayer has indeed been answered or, quite often, as we saw in Chapter 2 with my heart problem, not answered as we'd hoped and yet in a more marvelous way still! I strongly recommend it.

KEEPING A PRAYER DIARY ✦ 173

A PROJECT

Whether or not you decide to keep a more permanent prayer diary or to include it with your daily journal (should you have one), try keeping a diary for a one-week period. After seven days, put it in a safe place and then take it out and reread it in three or four weeks. As the hymn already quoted in the last chapter says, it may surprise you what God has done.

PART FOUR

THE FINAL AIM

Those who forget,
who obscure or who cannot see the target,
are seldom likely even to come close.

Tom Harpur (*obiter dictum*)

X

WRESTLING WITH GOD

Jacob was left alone:
and a man [angel/God] wrestled with him until daybreak.

Genesis 32:24

———

That night, that year
Of now done darkness, I, wretch, lay wrestling
with (my God!) my God.

From *Carrion Comfort*,
by Gerard Manley Hopkins (1844–1889)

———

He that wrestles with us strengthens our nerves,
and sharpens our skill.
Our antagonist is our helper.

Edmund Burke (1790)

———

But God who is able to prevail,
wrestled with him, as the Angel did with Jacob,
and marked him; marked him for his own.

Izaak Walton (1593–1683),

commenting upon the great poet, John Donne (1640)

In recent years, surprisingly enough, there has been a great deal of public interest in the biblical book of Genesis: for example, a major Bill Moyers'TV series on PBS, several popular books, and a spate of articles in the top news magazines. This renewed and totally unexpected awakening of interest in Genesis is another symptom of the widespread spiritual quest going on in our time. It has very little to do, significantly, with the old controversies over Genesis between evolutionists and creationists, literalists and liberals. Instead, the focus of this phenomenon is on the archetypal nature of the great stories and religious myths found in Genesis and the light they throw on our understanding of God, ourselves, and the world today.

As the title of this chapter suggests, one of these timeless episodes throws considerable light on our entire spiritual journey, and, in particular, upon the nature and practice of prayer. I'm talking about the dramatic account where the patriarch, Jacob, wrestles with an angel. The angel actually turns out to have been God because the story ends with Jacob calling the name of the place, Peniel, which is Hebrew for "The face of God." He gives us his reason: "For I have seen God face to face, and yet my life is preserved" (Genesis 32:30).

In Genesis, God is said to have chosen many people to do his will and to begin what biblical theologians call salvation history (for the Jews, for Christians, and then for the whole world, according to Judeo-Christian understanding). Like those other biblical characters God chose, Jacob was, to say the least, a very imperfect human being. He remains forever a comforting personality because he so reminds us, at least in general, of ourselves and of our many weaknesses. He began life by being a "mamma's boy." As a youth, he was a passive, dependent person, totally reliant upon his mother. Indeed, for too much of his life, Jacob was far too easily manipulated by her favoritism and scheming. Pushed by her, he ended up cheating his brother, Esau, out of his rightful inheritance by practicing, among other things, a blatant deception on his blind father, Isaac. In fact, because of this (and all his tricky ways), he soon found himself with some serious enemies on his trail. At one point, he had just managed to avert a major catastrophe at the avenging hands of his very angry father-in-law, Laban, and Laban's sons – as told in chapter 31. But, immediately afterwards, in chapter 32, when the story of the night of wrestling begins, Jacob is once more gripped by terror. Word has come that now Esau, in spite of having been offered an extravagant gift of appeasement – flocks of goats, camels, cattle and donkeys – is also in pursuit of him and at that moment was coming to meet him with 400 of his retainers. He too is bent on pursuing revenge for Jacob's self-seeking deceptions.

With his usual, well-practiced cunning, Jacob has a strategy. He decides to split his large party of wives (two), slaves, livestock and trusted hired help into several "droves." He orders most of them to go ahead and to say, as they are met by Esau's hostile forces, that Jacob himself is coming to attempt reconciliation but that these (the selected livestock) are "a present sent to my lord Esau." The text is very candid about all of this. It says, "For he thought, 'I may appease him with the present that goes ahead of me, and afterwards I shall see his face; perhaps he will accept me.'" Jacob himself remained camped on the east bank of the Jordan River, near a notch in the hills where a small brook, the Jabbok, flowed westward into the Jordan.

Incidentally, I remember well how in December 1976, I stood on the hills on the West Bank of the Jordan at dusk one night while an Israeli guide pointed out the dip in the skyline on the opposite side where the Jabbok creek cut through. Three of us, including a *Toronto Star* photographer, were walking the 165 kilometers from Nazareth to Bethlehem for a Christmas series in the newspaper and an eventual book on the biblical trek of Joseph and Mary at the first Christmas (Luke's gospel). We slept each night at a different frontier kibbutz, half farm community and half military outpost.

Returning to the Genesis account, we are told, "So the present passed on ahead of him, and he himself spent that night in the camp." In the middle of the night, he got up, took his wives, his two maids, his 11 children, and everything else he had with him and sent them also across the brook to be part of the appeasement procession. Jacob then stayed behind, alone. What resulted was an extraordinary adventure.

The relevant passage begins with the following statements: "Jacob was left alone; and a man wrestled with him until daybreak." There is a seeming, enigmatic confusion in the text because of the word "man." I won't go into the whole scholarly discussion over this, but the full context makes it clear it is God ultimately with whom he struggles. For example, afterwards, his name is changed from Jacob to Israel, meaning, "one who has striven with God and has prevailed." Jacob himself says at the end of the struggle that he has "seen" God. Later on, the Bible, in another book, refers to this story about Jacob and says, "And with his strength he fought with God. And he fought with an angel and prevailed."

The text continues:

When the man saw that he did not prevail against Jacob, he struck him on the hip socket; and Jacob's hip was put out of joint as he wrestled with him. Then he said: "Let me go, for the day is breaking."

But Jacob said, "I will not let you go, unless you bless me." So he said to him, "What is your name?" And he said, "Jacob" [which means "supplanter" or "deceiver"]. Then the man said, "You shall no longer be called Jacob, but Israel, for you have striven with God and with humans, and have prevailed." Then Jacob asked him, "Please tell me your name." But he said, "Why is it that you ask my name?" And there he blessed him. So Jacob called the place Peniel, saying, "For I have seen God face to face, and yet my life is preserved." The sun rose upon him as he passed...limping because of his hip. Therefore to this day the Israelites do not eat the thigh muscle that is on the hip socket, because he struck Jacob on the hip socket at the thigh muscle (Genesis 32:24–32).

There is a very learned and detailed discussion of this and similar strange Genesis passages in a remarkable book called *The Hidden Face of God*, by Richard Elliott Friedman. His argument is summed up in this brief quote:"Obviously there is a confusion...concerning a seeming overlap between the deity and angels. But it is confusing only so long as we imagine angels as beings...independent or separate from God. These texts indicate angels are rather conceived of...as expressions of God's presence."[1]

My principal concern, however, is with the overall concept of wrestling with the divine which this heroic tale illuminates. If you read the whole cycle of Jacob/Israel stories in Genesis, especially the first part of the chapter in which the account of the wrestling is told, you quickly discover that, despite his failings, Jacob was very much a person whose life revolved around prayer. In other words, in spite of his obvious weaknesses and failures, he was also a God-centered, God-driven man. In a lengthy prayer before the encounter with the strange man/angel/God, he pleads for deliverance from his brother and several times reminds God of God's previous promises. He openly complains how it seems they aren't being fulfilled – or certainly won't be if Esau does him harm. It's no namby-pamby prayer in any way. In fact, it's another example of a prayer with "suction."

Obviously, Jacob did not *literally* "wrestle with God" at the Jabbok. Yet in the truest most profound way possible, he did – as we all must – wrestle, struggle, or contend with God. It was an indispensable part of his difficult, sometimes seemingly impossible hero's journey toward ultimate spiritual fulfillment and victory. Jacob was at a major crisis point in his life, one where he knew his real battle was not so much with an exterior challenge – a risky confrontation with his brother – but an inner one. He knew this would require a full facing-up to himself, a hard look at the "truth in the inner part" – his needs, his fears, his deepest flaws – in the face of the very Source of all Reality, the Ground of his life and of all creation. The story illustrates his determination not to let this confrontation with inexorable stress, panic, and terror escape *without extracting some kind of blessing from it.* "I will not let you go, unless you bless me," he tells the man/angel/God with whom he struggles.

Instead of misery, fear, and possibly even death, Jacob's theme is blessing here. He's not content with mere survival, with getting out of this mess by the skin of his teeth, so to speak, through the use of further frauds and tricks. Like the substance addict who finally hits the low spot when the time has come for an end to all excuses, bravado, and struggling by oneself, Jacob knows his helplessness. He recognizes that he's ultimately dealing, not with this or that problem or enemy, but with "A Higher Power, with God," and that it is through that Source alone that his promised future can be realized.

The story is so rich in meaning and spiritual symbolism that one could easily go on for a very long time analyzing it and reflecting upon it. Indeed, I strongly suggest rereading this entire cycle of Jacob stories as a form of meditation regardless of one's religious background. The same of course is true regarding the Hindu scriptures, especially The Upanishads and The Bhagavad-Gita, or other holy books such as the Qur'an. It's a most liberating experience to find how one can be spiritually enriched by the sacred texts of all faiths. In my view, however, Jacob's night of wrestling is not meant to be taken as symbolizing a once-in-a-lifetime experience. It is readily apparent as you read his whole story that this episode makes vivid what was really an ongoing, neverending "wrestling" of Jacob's soul with its Maker. So it is, or can be, in our lives, too.

Two key aspects of this story are particularly relevant to any fresh discussion of prayer and so should not be ignored. The first is that this kind of conscious soul-wrestling, this kind of praying, has enormous power to change us as well. It does bring a "blessing," however bleak or terrifying our circumstance may be. It changes things; it changes people. The great mystics, saints and heroes of all the major approaches to spirituality all bear testimony to this truth. The ongoing struggle brings greater intimacy with God. The soul is enlarged and grows in maturity. Notice how Jacob's name is changed as an external symbol of these inner transformations and of his assured future of service to others. He is called Israel. Instead of "trickster" or "the one who supplants and robs others of their heritage," he is to be Israel, the founding father of the Israelites. As "Israel," his name denotes one who has risked total confrontation with God and yet has prevailed. This great, transforming crisis is an archetype, paradigm, or example to all of those who would later seek to follow the same spiritual path.

But notice second that, blessing or not, Jacob walked with a limp forever after this life-changing encounter. He had been "marked" as God's own, as Izaak Walton described it in the quote at the beginning of this chapter. The mark was one of a wound or trauma to his hip that he endured in the course of the all-night struggle.

Cliché or not, gain and pain are as indivisibly linked in the world of the spirit as they are elsewhere. Nobody would directly compare his or her spiritual journey to the Patriarch's or indeed to that of any of the spiritual greats of past or present. Yet the more books on spirituality I encounter, the more biographies of "saintly" men or women that I manage to read, the more it is evident that wrestling with God is one of the most dramatic and, at the same time, realistic and accurate descriptions of true prayer to be found anywhere. There often can be – even, it seems, must be – inexorable sweat, strain and pain involved, plus the risk of being wounded or "marked" as God's own if one is truly seeking her.

For Christians, the supreme example is in the gospels. In the Garden of Gethsemane, as Christ prayed for the "cup" he was about to drink to be removed from him, Luke tells us, "In his anguish he prayed more earnestly, and his sweat became like great drops of blood falling down on the ground." One of the greatest weaknesses of a good deal that passes for spiritual nurture today is found in the fact that it involves, in reality, a sort of "junk food" approach. It's too easy and too superficial. It has no "cross," no wrestling, no sweat, no "marking" – and, in the end, little sense of bite on one's true inner needs.

Others have developed the "wounded healer" theme elsewhere. But it is certainly the predominant note in the story of Jesus. Thomas asks specifically to see Jesus' "marks" or wounds.

Early legends and stories are full of the mythical importance (in Joseph Campbell's sense of the centrality and truth of myth) of the noble hero, savior, or adventurer, who wrestles with and overcomes both gods and wicked adversaries, but who is himself or herself hurt or "marked" indelibly in the process. One thinks, for example, of Frodo, in J. R. Tolkien's *The Lord of the Rings*. Frodo finally overcomes all obstacles and wins "salvation" for everybody else by renouncing and throwing the ring of power into the great cauldron of fire in the Land of Mordor. In his struggles, however, he receives a mark or wound while in mortal combat with his huge and horrible adversary, the spider Shelob. True, he manages to kill Shelob. But it is not before the huge monster has bitten Frodo on the neck. Like Jacob who limped everafter, Frodo also carried the scars and the deep inner wound for the rest of his life. Of course, the difference from the Jacob story was that Frodo's struggle was not with God but with this spidery symbol of evil.

GOD AS A "CONSUMING FIRE"

All this talk about marks or wounds, pain and sweat, and the metaphor of wrestling in prayer itself – the idea that the spiritual quest can involve times of great struggle or dry desert known as the "dark night of the soul" – runs heavily against popular wishes for a quick-fix, takeout kind of spirituality, where the easy path and the end gift promise to provide nothing but bliss, bliss, bliss. Many readers, therefore, may be surprised, even put off, by what I have just written. This, however, is largely because of a big misunderstanding. All the major faiths, as Scott Peck points out at the very beginning of his bestseller *The Road Less Traveled*, lay stress on the same truth: life itself is difficult and the spiritual life is in many ways the most difficult of all. The Buddha said it; Jesus said it; and so have a host of others in various

ways. Liberal Christians as well as those of other faiths sometimes get so carried away with their emphasis on God's
"cuddliness" that they miss this very important element.

Certainly Christians and most world faiths believe in a God
of love and mercy, but true love is not simply a wishy-washy,
divine "putting up" with our eternal, human propensity for
mediocrity, or for our frequent, sheer perversity. In his final pur-
poses, God really has our ultimate, best interests at heart. It's that
kind of "tough love" that's at stake whenever the divine compassion is considered with intelligence and honesty, instead of
with wishful thinking. That's why there are those otherwise totally opaque and enigmatic passages in the New Testament such
as "Our God is a consuming fire," and "It is a fearful thing to fall
into the hands of the Living God."

It's also why in the Hindu form of Trinitarian thought, God
is one, but there are three key aspects: Brahma, the Creator;
Vishnu, the Sustainer; and Siva, the Destroyer or Consumer. In a
spiritual sense, Siva can be invoked by Hindus to "consume" or
"destroy" the negative parts of one's personality and soul, the
blocks that interfere with our union with God.

Recently, I heard a leading Canadian yoga teacher – a man
of about 55 or 60, white, and educated in the Western world –
saying he mainly directs his prayers to God conceived of as Siva,
and asks particularly for the destruction of ignorance and other
dark features of his soul, such as hard-heartedness, selfishness,
and all the rest. Similarly, people trying to be truly committed
Christians often welcome the "fire of God's Spirit" as a cleans-
ing, refining power – the power of holiness or of inner and
outer wholeness.

Whether one uses the imagery of wrestling or of mystical
fire, the intent is ultimately the same: significant change for the

better, genuine spiritual growth. In other words, a spiritual life, a life of prayer, is not a comfortable, cosy, "safe-in-the-arms-of-Jesus" kind of experience. It can hurt. But any other way, though seemingly softer and more pleasurable, will in the end disappoint and rob the soul of its true joy. We were not made to be the abject slaves of our senses or of our lower selves. We can never be finally satisfied with the selfish quest for security; pure ease; or mindless, spiritless comfort. Such a quest only produces heart-loneliness, frustration, and a haunting emptiness inside – the precise feelings behind so much of the malaise in the most highly developed countries of the world today. You can read it almost everywhere in the writings of those who have done much research and given much thought to the human condition. From the late Mother Teresa, in India, to leading cardiologist, Dean Ornish, in California, the message is the same: Our real problem, especially in the rich, so-called developed countries, is a "spiritual heart disease," a malaise of the soul.

A POSSIBLE MISUNDERSTANDING

Before leaving this discussion, there is one possible misunderstanding I would like to try to anticipate and challenge. What has just been described as "wrestling with God" is a true and necessary way of experiencing prayer. But a caution needs to be given. Ancient classical wisdom always emphasized the need for balance; "nothing to excess" was the proverbial way of putting it for the Greeks. Eastern religions, in some cases for millennia BCE, have always taught the need for a balance of energies – the *yin* and the *yang*. The life of prayer is not *always* one of constant wrestling. An overemphasis on the struggle for its own sake could become a kind of deadening, spiritual masochism. There are times when one has wrestled enough for the moment and urgently needs to pause and rest. I have a wise professor friend who in the course of a recent, wide-ranging discussion about prayer told me he often arrives at a point in the "wrestling" when he realizes he is weakening and lacking in the energy to fight on. He told me, "At times, I simply have to make an act of trust and put it all in God's hands. I'm forced to 'let go and let God,' as some have put it, because it's just too much for me."

The truth is that there's a sort of rhythm to it all. There's a time to withdraw from the battle a little and to realize that our spiritual health requires frequent periods of simple relaxation in the confidence that the Higher Power is ultimately in charge and knows our need. You can see this rhythm in the life and ministry of Jesus in the gospels. "Come apart and rest a while," he tells his disciples. In one piece of narrative from the tradition, he and the disciples are out on the Sea of Galilee in a small boat. Jesus, we are told, was asleep, even though the wind and waves were rising and the boat was being tossed around. The gospels make it plain in numerous places that it was his habit to seek out places of solitude for meditation and quiet. There is a similar pattern in the lives of saints, gurus, and mystics in other religions. There is a time to pray and to wrestle and there is a time not to pray overtly at all, but just to rest or relax in God.

FOR REFLECTION AND ACTION

1. Are there some specific, unresolved issues right now in your life? Make a list of these and, using the simplest, most honest and searching words/thoughts you can muster, bring them into the Presence of the Divine Light, symbol of life's High-

est Power. Wrestle with God about them, not in an attempt to persuade or convince God to act in a particular way or to give a specific "answer," but in a sincere effort to get the whole truth out between you both and to find the strength and the illumination you need to move ahead. Always add a brief thanksgiving for past victories in either solving problems, learning to live with them (like Paul with his "thorn-in-the-flesh") or in transforming them, getting a blessing instead of total failure. As the hymn that begins, "It is no secret what God can do," aptly puts it: "What he's done for others, he can do for you..." Give thanks now in faith.

2. Write down certain attributes or aspects of your inner life which you realize are negative or need to be changed in some way. Acknowledge them fully as your own. Then visualize your inner self being flooded by Divine Light, by Divine Fire, or other consuming agent. See clearly the unwanted, dark qualities being destroyed, mopped up, cleansed or wholly transformed by the alchemy of God. Again, give thanks in anticipation of living – perhaps immediately, perhaps rather slowly – the results of this in your daily life.

XI

THE ULTIMATE GOAL
OF PRAYER

The day will come when,
after harnessing space, the winds, the tides and gravitation,
we shall harness for God the energies of love.
And, on that day, for the second time in the history of the world,
we shall have discovered fire.

Teilhard de Chardin S.J. (1881–1955), priest and scientist

―――――――

Therefore it is necessary to pray –
the fruit of prayer is deepening of Faith –
the fruit of Faith is Love – Love in action is service –
and so acts of love are acts of Peace –
and this is the living of The Golden Rule.
Love one another as God loves each one of us.

Mother Teresa, from the cover of *Oneness:*

Great Principles Shared by all Religions, by Jeffrey Moses[1]

*"Through appreciation of the wisdom of the past,
through prayer, and most of all, through deep meditation,
we can become one with the inner silence that is a part of God."*

From *Oneness: Great Principles Shared by all Religions*

by Jeffrey Moses

—————

*Set your priorities. Do not delay that which is most important.
You can know God now, but you can never know Him tomorrow.
Your enlightenment is the one thing you cannot postpone.*

God is now.

From *The Dragon Doesn't Live Here Anymore*

by Alan Cohen[2]

We have now considered many dimensions of this multifaceted reality called prayer. The subject is vast, however, and the aim throughout has been to be as concise and practical as possible without ignoring or skimping on anything essential. Therefore, I want to turn and focus attention now on the single most important question that can be asked in any human endeavor – that of ultimacy: "What is it in the whole matter of prayer that is really ultimate or final?" In other words, "What is the consummate end or goal of all our praying? Is there anything here for the sake of which we do everything else?" Readers of my syndicated column in the past know that I follow in this approach the teaching of a former clerical professor of mine. He did his students a great service by insisting that in all affairs, ethical, spiritual or whatever, greater clarity of thought can always be gained by asking two fundamental questions: one, "What is ultimate in any given endeavor or situation?" and two, "What does it mean to be fully human in the particular circumstances being considered?"

Of course, we pray in order to have the wisdom and the strength to cope with the challenges and difficulties of life. We pray for health, our own and that of loved ones and others. We pray for peace, for justice, for good government, for victims everywhere, for many thousands of things, events and situations. Most of this we have already looked at.

But prayer, obviously, is not just about our basic wants, needs, hopes and fears – however altruistic and far-reaching its scope may be in the final conclusion. It's ultimately about growing into an intimate relationship with the One in whose image we have been created. It's about enlightenment, about finally awakening to who we really are and to our total unity with God, with all other living beings, and with the seemingly inanimate parts of the cosmos as well – the sky, the seas, lakes, rivers, mountains, and winds. It cannot be stressed too much. The ultimate, the final goal of prayer is cosmic consciousness, a profound and for most a new awareness of the nature of, and reasons for, living; a loving oneness with God (who is herself the essence of love), with others, and with all that is.[3]

"Cosmic consciousness" is but one way of putting it. Various religions, traditions, and cultures have now, or have had in the past, different names for this kind of blissful experience, this radical transformation of consciousness. Plotinus (c.205–270 CE) described it as the "flight of the alone to the alone." Nevertheless, the experience makes one feel totally one with everything – liberated, enlightened, mystically united with the Divine. For those who are familiar with the more spiritual teachings (sometimes wrongly called esoteric, as though reserved for a very few) of all the great religions, this will already be a well-known concept, even if it hasn't been *experienced* yet. But it needs to be described here in some detail because the great majority of people in the Western world – and not least those committed to some form of Christianity – are ignorant of this core truth of the very religious tradition in which they or their parents and grandparents were raised.

Fear of such words as "mysticism" and a grossly overemphasized doctrine of human depravity, sin, and hence on the urgent need for individual "redemption" have warped the Christian message badly in my view. (Historically, the latter doctrine certainly gave the churches enormous power over their various flocks.) My research and thought over the years have convinced me that those thinkers and religious scholars who maintain that there is a universal nucleus of truths common to all major faiths are absolutely correct. This nucleus includes, principally, this idea of an experienced, higher level of consciousness – called union with God and all creation – as the ultimate goal of all spiritual practices. I have found that the closer the various religions come to their own centers, the closer they inevitably come to this core experience. This includes Christianity, Judaism, and Islam. If only they could agree on these fundamentals and then agree to disagree on all the rest – which remain largely a part of the wrappings anyway – what a different world it would be!

By the way, the story about the "wannabe-mystic" who asked the hot-dog vendor to "make me one with everything" certainly carries a questionable joke. Nevertheless, the anecdote articulates the essential point of praying and the quest for God. All the major faiths, with the possible exception of the strictest form of Buddhism (Theravada Buddhism), teach

1. that there is an Ultimate Reality or Ground of Being, called God – a God who is not a "Person" but who is definitely personal and who has created the cosmos;
2. that it is possible to know and to experience union with this personal, Spiritual Source; and,
3. that the entire purpose of life is to seek to do so.

This "perennial philosophy," as it has been called, is expressed at the heart of Christianity just as it is in one of, if not *the*, world's oldest religions, Hinduism. We have already seen something of this in discussing the apostle Paul's focus, which moved in his own letters from Jesus' emphasis upon the Kingdom of God in the synoptic gospels to that of believers being *en christo* or in Christ – what Albert Schweitzer called "the mysticism of Paul" in his famous 1930 book of the same name. Schweitzer, of course, argued that because Paul taught and insisted upon Christ's role as the sole mediator of union with God, Paul's view of God-union was different from other kinds of God-mysticism familiar in the ancient world. But this can be debated and is ultimately a form of unnecessary theological quibbling in my view. The similarities are much greater than the differences when you take a larger, more universal perspective.

In previous quotes from Romans chapter 8 we have seen how prayer itself is the work of God in the human heart. Without becoming unduly academic or theological here myself, I would have to say that, on any fair reading of his letters, Paul plainly both believed and taught that the final spiritual goal is to be at one, in the deepest possible unity, with God and that, one day, all the created order will share in the bliss of such a final consummation. In the end, even Christ himself will be "subjected unto the one who put all things in subjection under him [God], that God may be all in all" (1 Corinthians 15:28).[4] Study of Paul's understanding of the work of God's Spirit in our evolutionary development towards being "fellow-heirs" with Christ and "fellow-workers" with God shows clearly that, for Paul, to grow spiritually is to grow in knowledge of our unity with God until one day we see God "face to face."

WHAT JESUS TAUGHT

One of the curiosities of the New Testament is the way in which the gospel with the highest view of who Jesus was and is, at the same time insists not only on his full humanity but also upon our own divinity and our calling to realize our unity with God. For a fuller discussion of the differences between John's gospel, to which I'm referring, and the earlier three, I direct readers to my earlier book *For Christ's Sake* and to the numerous commentaries on John, most particularly that by the noted Roman Catholic scholar, Raymond Brown.

When you look at John's account from the perspective of the perennial philosophy, cosmic consciousness, or self-realization through awareness of union with the Divine, however, the similarities are extremely striking and powerful. Just as other faiths, mainly Eastern, hold that there is an imprint, image, or part of the underlying Ground of Being or God in every person waiting to be discovered or realized – the *Te* in Taoism, the *Atman* in Hinduism, etc. – so too in John. The whole point of the introduction of the gospel (which begins, not with a nativity story like Matthew or Luke, but back "in the beginning" of time itself, thus giving the gospel a cosmic sweep from the start) is that the *Logos* or "Word" gives light to every person coming into the world. We are each of us an expression or incarnation of the light of God's Logos which, we are told, is another way of saying "God." John 1:1 reads: "In the beginning was the Word, and the Word was with God, and the Word was God."

For John, to become aware of Jesus' real nature and to follow his Way to Ultimacy is to become aware of our own true nature as "children" or sons and daughters of God. It is only in John, for example, that Jesus points out to his critics that he is doing nothing unusual in hinting or saying that he is God's Son. To prove the validity of his teaching on this, he quotes to the crowd some very loaded words from the Hebrew Bible – which his rigid opponents claim "cannot err" – in which the whole of the Jewish people are called the "sons of God" or "children of the most high" (John 10:33–36 cf. Psalm 82:6). If they were all once called this by an infallible source, Jesus asks, what's the big fuss about when he uses the term to describe himself?

Those who want to make a vast gulf between Jesus Christ and the rest of humanity – the direct opposite of Christ's own apparent intention (which is why he repeatedly refers to himself in the synoptic gospels as "the Son of Man") – like to quote the passages where John has Jesus saying that he and "the Father" are one. This, they allege, is proof of his unique claim to divinity. But, unfortunately for that argument, he's obviously not making unique claims for himself here. Jesus, even in this passage and in John in general, is not claiming to be the Second Person of the Holy Trinity, as many conservatives would have us believe. He's simply stating what he had experienced as one who had become enlightened or who had realized his real nature. He knew what it was like to have realized his essential oneness with God.

The stories of his baptism in the Jordan River, found in their various forms in each of the four gospels, plainly mark the moment of Jesus' own enlightenment. From that point, he ceases to follow John the Baptist and begins his own ministry. The account of his trials and solitude in the wilderness for 40 days after the baptism points out the uniqueness of what this breaking in of cosmic consciousness at Jordan truly was and how he needed time alone to assimilate the new experience.

This kind of assertion about his deep sense of unity with the "Father" is the natural fruit of the kind of cosmic consciousness I have been describing. It's meant for everybody and, one day, at a higher stage of consciousness than we are now as a species, all humans will have it as naturally as we now have self-reflective awareness or the power to see in color. We will all one day realize our essential oneness with God. Jesus was and is, as the writer of The Letter to the Hebrews saw, one of the great pioneers or forerunners in this quantum leap forward. Writing in *Unity Magazine*, Eric Butterworth says the following:

This was the beginning of the "Age of the Christ," the "Divinity of Humankind." Up to this point, humans have existed in the consciousness of separation from God. We could pray to God, we could talk to God, and receive help and guidance from God. But God was always "out there" and humans were "down here." Now Jesus knew what the Psalmist had implied when he said: "Be still, and know that I am God!" in Psalm 46. Now he knew himself to be an expression of God, or the activity of God – life and intelligence [the Logos] pressing itself into visibility. Now he knew that the Kingdom of God, the wealth of the universe, was within the depth-potential within him.[5]

Though it may well seem heretical to fundamentalists and others, Jesus was and is not alone in the quantum leap. Though it seems abundantly apparent that Jesus was called or sent to be a special, even unique "Agent" or Emissary of the Divine, there have been and certainly will be others with a similar, mystical "Christ Mind." Paul, in fact, boldly claims that all Christian believers have the mind of Christ already, even though church history, with its accounts of Christian crusades, inquisitions, and other terrible acts, has failed to confirm this ideal. But one day, all humanity will arrive at a vast denouement of history, at what Teilhard de Chardin called the Omega Point, the goal of evolution, the ultimate unity of all human consciousness with God.

It is irrelevant here to discuss who amongst the founders, leaders, seers, prophets, mystics and saints of all Earth's various religions and spiritualities was "greatest" or most authoritative. I am a Christian, partly because of my background, but mainly because it is, for me personally, the path to Transcendence that seems most congenial and makes best sense. Many millions feel or see it all quite differently. By a "Christian" I mean one who accepts Jesus Christ as his or her Guru or Master pointing the way to God. Beneath the surface differences, all major paths to the Divine share a common experience and vision.Their original founders' conviction was that their experience ofTranscendence was meant for everybody.

The most compelling passage in the NewTestament dealing with union with God as the goal of prayer and the fulfillment of our purpose in being here also comes in John's gospel.The passage I have in mind wholly confirms the view that what Jesus experienced in his own life he intended and understood would be shared by those who followed him and his "Way." It occurs in the passion narrative, close to the very end of the gospel, on the very eve of his crucifixion. It constitutes the whole of chapter 17 and is generally referred to by interpreters as "The High-priestly Prayer" of Christ on behalf of his church. Every sermon I have ever heard on it and every scholarly book I have read so far has taken it as a prayer for the unity of all Christian people. It is always quoted at ecumenical gatherings and given this organizational or institutional "spin" – though little enough has been done about actual Christian unity down the centuries.

The truth is that read that way, with Christ as God, praying that his Church would be one, the prayer has to be considered to have been a near-total failure given the multitude of splits, divisions and creation of every kind of denomination imaginable. In other words, if you take the orthodox or traditional interpretation here, God's own prayer has not been answered! Right now, ecumenism itself, though some strides forward here and there have indeed been taken in the past few decades, is actually in the doldrums. There are even more divisions, denominations, and sects than ever before. I repeat, therefore, that the cause of church unity in some visible, institutional, or organizational form has been a serious disaster so far, if that is really what Christ was praying about.

Recently, however, I have come to the conclusion that this great prayer can and indeed should be read quite differently, that it should be read in terms of the unity-with-God experience which we are discussing. As we have seen, in all likelihood that was what Jesus discovered at the moment of his baptism in the Jordan – the illumination that the "Father" loved him unconditionally and that he was truly one with him as the child of God – and what he wanted his followers to have as well.

I don't propose to give a line-by-line scholar's treatment of the text. I simply ask you to reread John chapter 17 at your leisure and to make your own judgment. It is my conclusion that the central burden of this lengthy petition, obviously a composition of the author but based upon some intimate conversations or experiences of a trustworthy source or sources, is Jesus' deep longing for all his followers to know the unity with the "Father" that he had come to know. Repeatedly, he asks for his disciples and for those they will be preaching and ministering to "that they may be one, as we are one." In verse 21, he asks "that they may all be one. As you, Father, are in me and I am in you, may they also be in us, so that the world may believe that you have sent me" (in other words, realize through this experience that his message is authentic and true). Principally, Jesus is talking here about knowing oneself to be at one with God. A true sense of oneness with others of a like mind, and eventually with the whole of humanity, then follows naturally as day follows night.

This has little, indeed nothing, to do with some kind of institutional or hierarchical unity of Christian denominations – or of all the world's religions either. That is never going to happen. Besides, the kaleidoscope of differing approaches to the Source are an added richness once their common core has been discerned. In my view, any dreamed-of union of the many hundreds of differing Christian denominations into a sort of superchurch is a petty ideal in any case when contrasted to the far greater, deeper oneness of all humanity that Christ, and his great apostle, Paul, had in mind.

As the prayer concludes, it is made clear that to be one with God, to have the illumination which Christ had experienced and which he wanted to share with all humanity, to be "in God," is to know oneself totally loved by the Divine Source of all Reality and to be filled with that love. To be one with God or the Ground of all Being, one with Divine Love, one with one another, and one with the cosmos itself – that is the ultimate goal, not just of this prayer, but of *all* praying or communication with the Author and Maker of our souls.

Thus enlightened, thus endowed with a soul that knows and lives its ultimate nature, we can carry this "Christ Mind" or cosmic consciousness, this heart and outlook of the Buddha, Krishna or the Christ – or of an all-embracing new spiritual awareness – out into the needs, joys and problems of our daily lives and of the world around us. It is actually not important what we call it. Its universality and the transformations it inevitably causes are what truly matter. It brings a fresh vitality and energy to our inmost being that is instantly reflected in our bodies as well. The links between increased spirituality and vastly improved health and well-being afford one of the most exciting areas of medical research now and for the forseeable future. But the sure proof that this "Christ Mind" is ours comes in its outworking in thoughts and acts of greater compassion and self-giving on behalf of others, including the natural world which lies so badly wounded and degraded almost everywhere. Life begins to glow with a meaning and focus rarely even glimpsed before. Ralph Waldo Emerson once said, in speaking of its matchless value, that "The knowledge that this Spirit, which is essentially one, is in one's own and in all other bodies, is the wisdom of one who knows the Unity in all things."

In an intriguing 1996 article on the works of Emerson and his visionary thinking about the oneness of the entire cosmos, Steven Patascher, a noted and innovative scientific researcher from Scottsdale, Arizona, quotes scientist Hugo Munsterberg: "Our time longs for a new synthesis...It waits for science to satisfy our higher needs for a view of the world that shall give unity to our scattered experience."[6] This is a true-enough observation. However, it's my conviction that, while science is currently moving much closer to the realm of the Spirit through the impact of quantum physics and its increasing corollaries, we make a mistake in looking to it to solve our problem here. Science can certainly help. But the ultimate answer will not be a scientific hypothesis from the mind of humanity, but a spiritual experience from the heart. One day, as I and others now predict – and perhaps much sooner than we have so far intuited – it will belong to everyone. Meanwhile it begins with individuals like you and me.[7]

As R. M. Bucke once wrote, "When we are in tune with a consciousness of the cosmos, we become members of a new species." The evolution of humans is still incomplete, but the next and probably the last "quantum leap forward" is drawing near. Each of us has a part to play – by seeking God's kingdom within, by seeking its establishment in our own community and in the world. "Strive first for the Kingdom of God," said Jesus, in The Sermon on the Mount, recorded in Matthew. God, or if you prefer, the Cosmos, will do the rest.

A PRACTICAL PROJECT

If the final goal of all our praying is a deeper intimacy and unity with God, then it follows that all our prayers can and should ultimately be made from that perspective. Try making it a practice to reflect, if only for a few moments each day, upon this truth: we are, each one of us, directly and immediately connected not only with one another and with all other living things, but with everything that is – with the vast sweep of all creation and with the living, sustaining reality of the Divine. Simply meditate upon this and reaffirm its solid reality as a fact. One of the very best times to do this is when you are having or have just had one of life's "peak experiences," to use Maslow's term. Or perhaps when you are simply remembering one such moment in particular – a special moment of ecstasy or exaltation, an unexpected high gained from nature, special music, other art forms or whatever constitutes your greatest and deepest heart's desire. Such rare moments, life's best or "highs" in the fullest sense, already take one out of a narrow self-awareness towards and into a more cosmic awareness or consciousness. Seeing this, consciously feeling it, and then allowing yourself to be lost in it, even briefly, is to enter the threshold of the mystic's world. We are not alone; we are ultimately one with the totality of being and with the source of all energy and joy.

XII

SOME KNOTS UNTIED AND SOME CONCLUSIONS REACHED

All things are of one pattern made,
Bird, beast, and flower, ...deceive us,
Seeming to be many things
And are but ONE.

Ralph Waldo Emerson (1803–1882)

————

The Divine comes in its own time.

Swami Radha, *Time to be Holy* (p.24)

————

We shall not cease from exploration
And the end of all our exploring
Will be to arrive where we started
And know the place for the first time.

T. S. Eliot, *Little Gidding*, 1942, Prt. 5

———————

What we call the beginning is often the end
And to make an end is to make a beginning.
The end is where we start from.

T. S. Eliot, *Little Gidding*, Prt. 5

SOME KNOTS UNTIED

HOW DOES PRAYER REALLY WORK?

This matter came up in the very first chapter of the book, near its conclusion. But it is important at this point to repeat and to expand somewhat on what was written there.

The truth is that, in spite of the ongoing research I referred to briefly at the beginning, we don't know yet and perhaps we never will – at least while we remain in this earthly dimension of existence – how prayer works. By "we" I include, of course, many living masters of prayer who are much farther along the spiritual road than any of us. However, that it does indeed "work" I myself know for a certainty from the most convincing evidence of all to me as an individual – the experience of a lifetime with prayer, my own and that of others. It's a little like the whole matter of spiritual healing. In my investigations for *The Uncommon Touch*, I quickly discovered a considerable amount of hard data revealing that such healing can be shown to have positive results, even under the strictest of laboratory conditions – with double-blind, randomized conditions and all the other protocols demanded by scientific researchers. But, again, while more research goes on and more evidence accumulates of healing having taken place, the mechanism or explanation of how it happens or why remains quite elusive.

We should not be dismayed or held back from actual practice by the amount of mystery in either case. Take our uniquely human self-reflective awareness or consciousness, for example. Consciousness studies are in full spate just now and will be for the foreseeable future. It seems obvious to even the most unskilled in such a field that the questions of how consciousness came into being, what it truly is, and how it operates, hold the key to some of the greatest "knots" or riddles in the universe. Perhaps, as many sacred scriptures suggest — including, for example, the Vedic writings of Hinduism and the Bible itself — consciousness has always existed from the first. So the material world, our physical brains as well, arose out of it. The brain, then, which is a specific form of matter, would not, nor would any other kind of matter, be the originator of consciousness, but its tool — a sort of transformer or adaptor for a cosmic reality, consciousness, which is all around us. As yet, however, even the experts on this admit they, together with leaders in many other research areas, are like children playing on the beach of a vast and as yet unexplored continent.

Certainly, as I suggest in *The Uncommon Touch*, there is some subtle kind of consciousness involved in prayer, in addition to what we ourselves are aware of; there is some kind of energy-plus-information transfer going on, but it is totally unlike anything science presently knows. The mystery, I repeat, doesn't bother me. Science cannot now and probably never will be able to explain the deepest things pertaining to God and God's relationship with all that is, including our species. Science, however, especially since the dawning of quantum physics, is increasingly an ally here and not a foe. As Albert Einstein said in his book *Out of My Later Years*, "Science without religion is lame, religion without science is blind."[1]

I recently read an article, in a scientific journal called *The Equator*, by noted scientists Robert G. Jahn and Brenda J. Dunne — the authors, among many other works, of the 1987 book *Margins of Reality: the Role of Consciousness in the Physical World*.[2] The piece I'm referring to, titled "The Spiritual Substance of Science," described in considerable detail the continuing experiments at

Princeton University. These experiments – begun in 1979 – attempt to establish whether or not human consciousness, by deliberate intention, by pure thought alone, can alter in any way the working of simple random-event machines. The project is called PEAR (Princeton Engineering Anomalies Research program) and has involved well over 100 uncompensated volunteers, including many sceptics, from all walks of life. The studies themselves have been designed by a broadly interdisciplinary staff from psychologists, engineers, and physicists to professors in the humanities. There has been some brief mention of PEAR in the press from time to time, but Dunne and Jahn's article is the first full-length review of the results that I have seen.

Summarizing PEAR's findings, one can say unequivocally that the project to date, involving nearly 2.5 million computerized trials, "strongly indicates" that human consciousness – as it exchanges information with its environment – orders it, and interprets it as well. Human consciousness "has the ability to bias [alter] probabilistic physical events." In other words, it can actually move or change certain "margins of reality" to a significant degree by the simple intention of doing so. In addition, other PEAR human/machine experiments have shown that human consciousness can succeed in affecting the random results of machines operating at remote points several thousand miles away! The article says, "In fact, one of the most fascinating features of all of this anomalous experimental evidence is its remarkable insensitivity to the magnitude of the distance separating the operator from the machine or, in the case of the perception of very distant objects or sites, the remote percipient from his target."

None of this "proves" anything about prayer. But it does show in an amazing and intriguing fashion that there are modes of information transfer and other powers of human consciousness – working both close up and at huge distances – that science never before even dreamed of. Professor Rupert Sheldrake's work at Cambridge University on what he calls "morphic resonance," a newly discovered kind of telecommunication between animals and between humans, is also relevant here. Still, the power of prayer is analogous to, but, in my thinking, far greater than any of these.

DOES IT MATTER TO WHOM ONE PRAYS?

This is not really a question about seemingly competing gods or religions. All faiths can mediate or witness to the one Ultimate Transcendent Reality we call God. None can possibly contain God or claim to have the monopoly of truth about the Divine Mystery, despite what the true believers say. God is not a Christian, God is not a Hindu, nor a Muslim, Jew, or Sikh. It is certainly not a question of choosing between God as male and a "Goddess" of some kind who is obviously female. Because God is so far beyond anything or anyone we can define precisely or fully comprehend, a reality so numinous or "otherly" that even a glimpse of the full glory would overwhelm us utterly, we are of necessity forced to find images and symbols or more human-like deities, saints, and gurus to pray through or to ask in the name of. I believe, however, that there is an important distinction to be made here. One can indeed pray through or in the name of any one of a host of God-revealers (that is, according to one or another of the highest of the many revelations of the Divine), be it Moses, Jesus, Krishna or perhaps the name of some sacred symbol such as The Light. But the ultimate One being prayed to is God.

For example, though many Christians pray to Jesus, he himself, in the only records we have, the gospels and epistles, never taught or advised those who would be disciples (learners) of his Way to pray in such a manner. He was always careful to direct his own and others' prayer to God alone. Certainly he is quoted in the gospels as often referring to praying "in my name," in other words, in accordance with his teaching, ministry, and loving revelation on God's behalf. But he wouldn't allow the rich young ruler even to call him "good master" let alone pray to him! Rebuking the rich young man, Jesus said, "No one is good but God alone" (Luke 18:19).

In Hinduism, there are many deities, symbolizing various energies of nature and different aspects of Divinity; but the ultimate object of prayer even there is the one God, Brahman. What seems on the outside to be polytheism is, at the heart, monotheism.

God alone, then, is the one to whom, with whom, and by whom we pray. Since, as I said at the start, our images and ideas of God are so inadequate and often tend to become fixed, even idolatrous, it has become my practice from time to time to preface my own prayers with something like this: "God, help me to pray to you, not as I think you are or as I picture you in my mind, but as you really are." I have shared this insight with readers before and whenever I speak about prayer, because it seems to me to be one of the most important lessons I have ever learned about the spiritual path. I forget now who first shared this particular prayer with me, but I have been greatly indebted to him or her for many years. I strongly recommend using it often because it will help anyone who does so to clarify both their heart and mind in approaching the One to whom all creation prays.

IS IT RIGHT TO PRAY FOR A "MIRACLE"?

A young married woman, who was responding to something I had said about prayer in a program on Vision/TV, wrote to me recently with this question: "Some people, myself among them, pray for an outcome to a problem or situation that in all likelihood won't happen, and when it doesn't they're disillusioned and think either that they have somehow failed or that there is no God after all. Do you think it's right to pray for a miracle?" Incidentally, she went on to say that, in the case of her and her husband, after trying every medical route to fertility known to science, they nevertheless still found themselves praying for a baby, a "miracle."

Since in my last book I tried to deal with the matter of miracles in depth, I won't repeat that all here.[3] It's enough to say that I take the position that the traditional sense of miracle, from the Latin *miraculum,* something that causes us to feel awe or wonder since it appears to contradict or reverse the way things usually are – an actual intervention in the laws of nature for the benefit of some individual or group – is based on a misunderstanding. Personally, I do not believe God breaks her/his own laws of nature as a special favor to anyone. I define a miracle, instead, as something that brings wonderment or even amazement because it has happened according to aspects of nature or of the entire cosmos which as yet lie partly or indeed wholly beyond our understanding. This is true of healing miracles or any other kind you can think of. The miracles of science and those which lie well beyond have this in common: they are caused by tapping into the way in which the universe actually works once you know the secrets. So while always praying for wisdom to know when to "let go and let God" (for example, in the case of a terminally ill person who because of pain and irreversible

injury or physical deterioration needs or desires the healing of
death), and while seeking to pray according to God's will, I believe we should not fear disillusionment but dare to pray for the
apparently impossible whenever our heart moves us to do so. As
Jesus pointed out, "With God, nothing is impossible."

We have already seen how such prayers can be answered in
ways far different from our assumptions or direct expectations.
This does not mean we have failed in any way or that "God is
dead." The answer may be "no" and may be so for our own and/
or others' good. This brings us back once more to the experience of "waiting upon God."

I'm reminded again of the sentences by Franciscan friar
Daniel P. Sulmasy, which I quoted at the end of the introduction
to this book. Dr. Sulmasy is the Director for Clinical Bioethics
at Georgetown Medical Center, Washington, D.C., and his book
is called *The Healer's Calling: A Spirituality for Physicians and Other
Health Care Professionals*.[4] He writes, "Prayer is often only the
experience of waiting. Prayer is sometimes nothing more than
the conscious experience of desire for God. It might not even
be a sense of the presence of God. It might be only darkness and
silence." Yet, as I said before, the witness of countless numbers
down the ages is that God is still in that darkness and silence and
ultimately will bless us and "put a new song" in our mouths,
"even a thanksgiving unto our God."

PRAYER AND SOCIAL JUSTICE:
IS THERE ANY CONNECTION?

Those critics who see all religion and all spirituality as forms of
escape from the so-called "real world" are often quick to label
prayer as a kind of self-indulgent, self-regarding, head-in-the-
sand ritual or practice. True prayer, however, is the total opposite

of this. The act of honestly communicating with the Creator and Sustainer of the Earth and all that is in it, the habit of baring one's soul to God and of earnestly seeking to do the will of God, inexorably does at least two vital things. First, it brings a renewed compassion and concern for other human beings, especially those facing want, pain, oppression, fear or any other dehumanizing condition. Prayer that doesn't do this is some form of idolatry and, in the end, a waste of time since it lacks a true vision of the nature of God. Second, regular and emergency-style prayer taps deeply into the energy and spiritual resources for carrying out the challenges of social justice at home and around the globe.

I was struck by the power of this connection time and again in my 12 years (1971–1983) spent traveling the world as the religion editor for *The Toronto Star*. When Bob Olsen, a *Star* photographer, and I spent several weeks in India and Nepal in the fall of 1979 for a series of front-page stories called "Christmas in Asia," we were privileged to interview and to spend considerable time in Calcutta with Mother Teresa, who had just won the Nobel Peace Prize. Visiting her "House of the Dying" in the precincts of a temple of Kali, her large and crowded orphanage, and watching the daily distribution of food to the starving, we were both struck with wonder that such a tiny, frail-looking person – a good wind could have blown her away – could do so much. In the years between our visit and her death early in September 1997, she was to go on and do so very much more, extending her mission to nearly 200 centers, including major cities in Canada and the United States. Her secret of strength, she said, was found in the worship, the prayers, which the community offered at crack of dawn each day and then once again just before retiring.

Almost everywhere I went in Asia, in Africa, in Central America, and in North American slums and ghettos, this same story repeated itself. The people who were not "cursing the darkness" but who were lighting candles of love and action were almost always persons of intense prayer. They weren't escaping from anything. They were up to their armpits in the struggle to change injustice and to make a new world. Moreover, though institutionalized religion and its often boring or rigid-seeming prayers can irritate or offend one, church, synagogue, or temple are the only places one can go to and be sure of finding some meaningful and collective way to relate to the otherwise unreachable tragedies and oppressions beyond our favored shores. They are one place where you can pray for the victims of the horrible events that shock us in the media every day. You can pray there also for those whom politicians, agencies, volunteers, and others are frantically working to relieve; you can pray to prevent such calamities from spreading; and you can give effectively of cash or other necessary services as a way of helping to provide material necessities as well. Prayer, then, is not at all about escaping, but about engagement with this wonderful yet terribly needy world. Never give in to the subtle yet ongoing temptation to quit.[5]

IF PRAYER IS SO POWERFUL, WHY NOT LEAVE EVERYTHING TO PRAYER?

Some very pious and often very good people have the same answer for every question or problem: "Go and pray about it." In my youth, it was a routine response from my parents, from their church friends, and from those they looked up to in the faith, to any and every worry or difficulty one had. I remember once telling my father that I was feeling quite depressed.

Instead of discussing it or recommending someone who could be of genuine help, he told me not to mention it to anyone but, above all, to pray about it. Many of those who read this book will have come from similar backgrounds and will recognize one's deepening feelings of near-despair in the face of such lack of either practical or spiritual wisdom – not to mention compassion.

Nowhere does the Bible, or the vast majority of sacred writings of all faiths which I have read, suggest that prayer is to be used as a substitute for personal effort, serious thinking, or positive action where it is needed. It is right to pray about everything. But to only pray about feeling low or depressed, for example, simply underlines and worsens the problem for both mind and soul. There is a time to stop praying about someone or something and to act.

Elsewhere, I have described some of the incidents which brought me from teaching New Testament and Greek in a small Anglican seminary at the University of Toronto to more than a quarter of a century in the mass media.[6] But the fact is that I will never forget the key turning point in that process and how it came about. I lived in the college with my family on the campus of The University of Toronto. One day, early in 1967, I was working in my study when someone knocked on my door. I went and opened it expecting to find one of my students with a question or perhaps an overdue essay to hand in. Instead, I saw an Armenian friend by the name of Albert Noradunkian. Albert belonged to an Armenian congregation, but he used to come to hear me preach at Little Trinity Anglican Church in downtown Toronto, where I was an assistant priest on Sundays. He was and is a delightful person to know, a sort of Renaissance man, a jeweler by trade, studying and

KNOTS UNTIED AND CONCLUSIONS REACHED ✦ 217

writing theology, making bread and wine, and willing to engage in witty conversation on almost any subject.

I asked Albert in, and, after some preliminary and typically
upbeat conversation, he suddenly became very serious. He said
he had been thinking a lot about me lately and that God had led
him to come and give me a message. Since I was at that time in
my life questioning whether or not a theological college was
where I wanted or was meant to be – in the 1960s so much was
going on out there in the real world beyond our walls, and so
much of theological training seemed incestuous, the church talking in obscure language both about and to itself – I was really
ready to hear what he had to say. He said, "God has told me you
should be out there communicating in the mass media." This
was a surprise indeed. One of the strongest desires in my deepest self, one which I could scarcely even bring to consciousness
for any length of time because it seemed at such odds with my
entire career to that point, was to be a writer in the press and to
somehow get into radio as well. Television was also soon to become a big part of my life, but I felt little attraction to it just
then. I told Albert how newspapers and radio had been in my
heart for a long time. "What are you doing about them?" he
abruptly enquired. I replied that I was praying about them and
about what I should do.

To my further surprise, he quickly blurted out, "Then it's
time to stop praying. Don't pray about it any longer. The time
has come to act." He illustrated his point by recalling the story
of the raising of Lazarus in John's gospel and of how Jesus told
some of the witnesses at the tomb to "move the stone." Albert's
argument was that if Christ could raise a man from the dead he
could also have "popped the stone off the tomb." But he refused
to do for others what they could do for themselves. Without

commenting from a scholarly viewpoint about whether the Lazarus story was historical and authentic or not, I saw his meaning. He went on to ask me how many editors, publishers, or owners of radio stations I knew personally. When I said none, he said, "Then move the stone! Take one or two of them out to lunch and get to know them; tell them of your dreams."

Next day, I remembered that I did know of an Anglican layman who was co-owner of a small country and western radio station in Richmond Hill, Ontario. I telephoned him, introduced myself, and suggested we meet sometime because I had an idea for a program. He promptly set a date for the following day and he came down to the college. By the time he left, we had agreed to try an open-line program – which the station soon decided to call "Harpur's Heaven and Hell." It was to begin not in the far-off fall, which was my suggestion, but in a week's time. When the press heard that a professor of theology was appearing on a radio station that played songs like *Drop-kick Me, Jesus, Through the Goalposts of Life* and other similar theological nuggets, stories appeared and then I was invited to write opinion pieces for *The Toronto Star's* religion pages. I remember one of the first I wrote was headed, "The gospel according to James Bond." Another, less popular in some quarters, was "Bishops – who needs them?"

In any event, the call to act in my dilemma over vocation and not just to pray about it was a huge turning point for me. Simple though his message was, I'll always be intensely grateful to Albert and to God's words through him. I wouldn't have missed for anything the adventures and excitement of the years since 1971 when the process initiated by Albert's visit was consummated and I finally left my professorship at the college and became a full-time journalist and a communicator in every kind of mass medium available at the time.

In Eastern spiritual thought, they speak of two kinds of approaches to grace or God's "lifting power" in response to prayer. I have written about them before.[7] There is the "kitten" understanding and there is the "monkey" approach. "Kitten grace" is where the believer takes the view that God alone does everything. "Pray about it" is the only necessary response to any situation. It all depends on God. The mother cat picks up her kittens one by one and carries them safely to wherever it is she decides they should be. You have seen it happen. The kitten does nothing except hang there helplessly while the mother does it all. "Monkey grace" is quite different. The mother monkey carries the full weight of her offspring as she climbs or swings precariously. In a sense, she does it all. Yet, at the same time, she does not. The observer quickly notices that the baby monkey is holding on for dear life. It knows that while all depends on mother, if the baby herself lets go, then she will fall. Her life could be destroyed. What this represents is a view of grace and of prayer in which God and humans work together in a form of synergy. God still remains sovereign in this view, yet our freedom, our cooperation, our extended best effort to bring about the object of our prayers are also required. Hence the seeming paradox of Paul's memorable words to the Philippians: "Work out your own salvation with fear and trembling; for it is God who is at work in you, enabling you both to will and to work for his good pleasure" (Philippians 2:12). As one of my favorite spiritual aphorisms puts it, "Act and work as though it all depends upon you; pray as though it all depends upon God."

WHAT ABOUT TEACHING CHILDREN
ABOUT PRAYER?

I have written before about children and spirituality in general.[8] The essence of what I wrote there is found in the statement that all children are potential spiritual geniuses. Their spiritual gifts, however, soon become forgotten in too many cases. Not recognized and so left without nurture, they get layered over and covered with the onrush of other pleasures and demands more dear to our culture. Obviously, children learn the most about the importance of prayer and how to set about it from their own parents in their own home. Children who see their parents pray through their words and actions, and who are led until age six or seven in learning some simple prayers, gain a foundation that will stand up well and develop as they mature. But it needs careful attention.

I do not, of course, mean thrusting prayer upon them as though it were a sort of medicine or even a punishment of some kind. One of life's most moving moments for a parent or other adult is to be present when a small child prays and to help them grow in it. But prayer done under coercion or wrapped about with unnecessary, pious unction, is about as unsatisfactory and counterproductive as any discipline or routine can be. The same is true of a prayer time before bed which is repeated with such sameness and such obvious haste that it becomes a purely mechanical rite like brushing teeth.

Most religious bookstores have books and other aids to help children learn how to pray. Whatever you do, you should be as aware as possible of what they love or fear the most, as well as be deeply respectful of their very real concerns for nature and for others in trouble or in need. Their openness and sensitivity are literally boundless – a tremendous trust and responsibility. Get them, as soon as they are interested in doing so, to suggest what they want to include in their prayers so that from the earliest moment they can see what prayer truly is – a conversation with the Source of life and of all creation.

One of the worst prayers to inflict on any child is one that just the other day a woman in her mid-30s told me, without a blush, she still prays: "Now I lay me down to sleep..." It includes the particularly unfortunate line, "And if I die before I wake, I pray the Lord my soul to take." I'm sorry to report that the same woman went on to describe her faith in a few sentences which revealed a spirituality stuck at about the same level as her only prayer. Why is it that so many of us expect to grow and to mature in every other way, but when it comes to things of the Spirit we're content to hold on to what Paul called "childish things"?

With regard to school and prayer, except possibly in the case of denominational or other religious schools, though even there I question it, it has long been my position that the act of prayer itself should not be imposed on anyone, especially on young students. True prayer is never the result of a process in which there is no choice. It can never really be imposed successfully from above. The farthest I would go in that direction would be in approving a very brief time of silence at the beginning of the school day in which those who wish to can pray or meditate while others who have no faith in God or spiritual practices simply quiet their minds or whatever. In other words, a moment for reflection, sacred or secular, completely left up to the individual.

Prayer, as a huge reality for millions of people throughout all of recorded time, should, in my view, be taught as part of an academic treatment of religion and spirituality. I am convinced that churches, other faith groups, or sects of various kinds should not receive public money for religious schools – as, for example, Roman Catholics now do in many parts of Canada. In fact, I believe that all children ought to receive the same kind of public education. But such an education would be – and where it now exists already is – fraudulent unless it included the kind of comparative religions, academic approach, given to all other important subjects. Nobody can call him or herself educated now without some basic understanding of the world's major faiths and of such key subjects as prayer.

I'm not usually a keen fan of Shirley Maclaine's New Age opinions, but I must say I was very struck by her courage and insight in a recent speech she made to a large gathering of media moguls in the United States. Her theme was that they were consistently missing the central story behind all the other stories they were publishing or broadcasting. She meant the importance of religion and spirituality in every significant event, ethical conundrum, or violent conflict in our world today.

For schools in our present multifaith, multicultural "global village," not to teach about mystical and spiritual traditions, rites, and core beliefs of the major religious communities is to promote an ignorance which is one of the basic conditions for intolerance and violence. Church, temple, synagogue and, above all, home – these are the places where the teaching of faith itself and of particular approaches to the Divine Light belong.

TOO TIRED TO PRAY?

A young businessman, who said he had recently married his childhood sweetheart, wrote to me recently in response to some things I had said about prayer on Skylight, which is the daily flagship, current affairs program on Canada's interfaith television network, Vision/TV. Among other queries, he spoke of one that I know affects everyone who attempts to pray, at least from time to time. He wrote, "I sometimes feel much too tired to pray at the end of the business day – and, I'm ashamed to admit, often even at the beginning. I've probably been over and over certain problems in my mind and just don't seem to have the energy to go over them again in prayer form. Do you think God knows that we intend to pray and won't ignore those of us who may need it most but who are too weary to ask for help?"

Earlier, I touched on this quite briefly, but it's important to speak about it again at the end. God knows the deepest intentions of our minds and hearts. Our innermost dialogues are always being heard. To desire to pray is in itself a prayer in the sight of God. I'm sure, for example, that at times Jesus himself, and all of the other spiritual leaders revered by humanity, knew this very human experience of being too bone-tired to pray, at least anything more than a quick "arrow" prayer. Prayer, I repeat, is often a sigh too deep for words in any case. As the famous yogi, Patanjali, once said, "Religion is not simply a state of euphoria. There will be relapses; phases of struggle, dryness and doubt...There is no failure as we continue to make an effort."[9]

On the other hand, if we begin to fall back on this line of thinking more and more frequently, it would be a good idea to take a closer look at the order and pattern of our use of both time and energy. It's one thing to realize that everything can be prayer; it's another to become extraordinarily and quite unnecessarily lazy. For example, in the case of this young man, the thinking about his problems which makes him reluctant to rehash them as prayers could be directly experienced by him as prayer itself. All he needs to do is to preface his inner thought and concerns with a brief, silent, honest prayer that he's worried about A, B, or C, and that as he thinks about them he would like to bring them to the Light. It's a tremendous help, if you're going to worry anyway, to ask God not just for illumination but for grace to think straight and to shirk from no aspect of the problem itself. When you get weary of that too, it's time to step back, express thanks for God's Presence in the process, and then leave the rest to the Divine.

When none of this is possible, when we are too fatigued, too sick in body or too down in our spirits for any formulation of thoughts or ideas, we can just be still, trust, and do nothing else at all. The "hidden fire" is always burning in our soul, and God, who is the very essence of love, knows this – since God put it there in the first place – and honors it with ceaseless compassion.

CAN PRAYER EVER HAVE NEGATIVE EFFECTS? CAN PRAYER DO HARM?

At first this may seem like a question one shouldn't even raise let alone think about and discuss in a book like this. But we must not avoid it simply out of a false piety or a wish to, as it were, protect God! Besides, Dr. Larry Dossey's new book *Be Careful What You Pray For – You might just get it* spends over 200 pages examining and expounding this very theme.

Your prayers, this leading researcher into prayer asserts, can do harm. Other people's prayers for you can do harm. Dossey, as we have seen, is pro-prayer, not anti. However, he's convinced that the same process that can produce positive results can intentionally or unintentionally achieve the opposite. In other words, there is a shadow or dark side to prayer. Dossey cites a 1994 Gallup Poll

according to which 5 percent of Americans said they have deliberately prayed for harm to come to others. There are such "hex-
prayers" out there, he argues, against which one needs some form
of "protection" or shield. But even those with good motives can
cause harm by seeking control of those prayed for, by praying
manipulatively in their own interests, and by all kinds of other
forms of improper interference in the lives of others.

He has put together an amazing amount of research and it
makes for a fascinating read. In spite of all this, I have some real
problems with Dossey's overall case. There is little doubt in my
mind that prayer used malignantly, capriciously, or solely in
terms of a person's selfish view that he or she really knows
what is best for other people, without reference to their innate
freedom and destiny under God, has real potential to rebound
negatively on the sender. It could harm the life and character
of the one doing the cursing and/or praying. But according to
Dossey's thesis, some prayer is dangerous; it is really not prayer
but a form of magic, or whatever, by which God or the universe is compelled to do hurt. This notion of prayer I can not
accept because it forces God to act against God's own nature –
which is infinite love.

The only prayers that can be answered, according to the law
of sovereign, divine love, are those which are in full harmony
with God's will for each of us. Any power that curses or hexes
may have, derives not from beyond human resources, but from
the force of deep belief in their efficacy held by the one or ones
being threatened.

Nevertheless, it is my experience that people can get very
confused and even badly misled by dwelling overmuch on supposed negative aspects of prayer. It is important to be self-aware
in praying or in being prayed for, just as it is in everything we

think and do. But it is equally important not to become obsessed or sidetracked by unlikely risks. Of course, even if such putative risks were real, they could easily be avoided by a couple of simple safeguards. (Indeed, Dossey himself recognizes and points to this truth at the conclusion of his study.)

1. We can protect ourselves against would-be malignant and all other possible kinds of well-meaning but unwelcome prayers (or curses) by a simple request to God – or The Mind of the Universe – each day for protection. The "deliver us from evil" in the Our Father is such a request in powerful yet simple form. Or, as Paul suggests, one can ask to be clad with "the armor of Light." Or one can assert daily, as in the Divine Light Invocation of Swami Radha, "I am being protected by the Divine Light."

2. We can avoid even a remote possibility of harming anyone by always asking that the will of God for the person or persons being prayed for be done. It's extremely important to know that The Ultimate Cosmic Wisdom, whom most people call God, knows the very best for all of us. Asking according to this Mind or Will automatically filters out both conscious and unconscious energies which could flow as a result of either our wrongheadedness or our simple lack of mindfulness. Praying to God in the name of Jesus or any other outstanding, universally recognized spiritual symbol or Persona, is another way to cancel out any potentially harmful agenda, whether recognized or not.

In short, by praying to be kept from all evil and by conditioning all our prayers with the proviso that God's will be done, any conceivable negative dimension of prayer can be discounted. We can get on with the real job at hand – that of lifting up others and ourselves into the Light

SOME CONCLUSIONS REACHED

THE PRODUCT OF A LIFETIME

In the evening of the day on which I completed the first draft of this manuscript, a friend I had not heard from for some time happened to call on the telephone. After we had talked for a while, he asked what I was working on at the moment and I told him about this personal book on prayer. He asked me how long it had taken me to write the rough copy. I heard myself saying, "About 10 or 11 months, I believe." But instantly, inside, at a much deeper level, a sort of still, small voice said to me, "It took so much longer than that. Actually, it has taken a lifetime." The first answer may have been right as far as it went; but the latter, the one I alone heard, told the real truth. In a sense, I have been working on it ever since as a student, long ago, I first began to wrestle with the idea and practice of prayer as it applied to my own life. As with all of us, I'm convinced God had been "working" on me since long before that again, indeed since childhood. The journey into God's Light never ends. Each seeming ending is actually always a new beginning, and, like most of you, in prayer and in so many other spiritual realms, I know full well that I still have very many "miles to go."

THE STRONGEST ARGUMENT

Reviewing everything I have said in this book, the strongest argument in favor of the reality and power of prayer, I believe, is that you can put it to the test and experiment with it for yourself. This book has not been principally about theory, but about heart and mind knowledge gained from one's own actual experience. By this route, prayer is discovered to be real and vital, not so much because of specific answers received, though I take back nothing of what has been said about that, but because of the way it transforms one's relationship with oneself, with the rest of the world, and with God. We find as we pray that we are indeed "wired for God," as Dr. Benson of Harvard has described it. It is deeply satisfying to know that what this modern research scientist is talking about in such a concise, summing-up phrase is precisely the same phenomenon believed in and so eloquently described by St. Augustine (354–430), more than 1,500 years ago, in these familiar words: "You have made us for Yourself, and our souls are restless until they find their rest in You."

THE ULTIMATE GOAL OF PRAYER REVISITED

In the end, the final goal of prayer and praying is not to discover or "prove" that such a practice is useful, practical, helpful, comforting, or any such thing – though it can be all of these and more. Ultimately, it is about discovering that God is already within us and bringing to full fruition what it means to be at one with the Source and Sustainer of everything that is.

Our frequent, extremely painful sense of isolation from one another is a fatal illusion – and harmful to the planet and all its other inhabitants. Prayer gradually reveals to us spiritually what modern physics has in its own way now shown to be fact: that there is a deep, underlying unity to the entire cosmos. We are, just by being here, a part of everything and everyone else. Beneath the obvious diversities lies an essential and universal unity that reaches to and beyond the farthest galaxy. We increasingly become aware, as we pray, that we belong in a special way to this unity because we have become conscious that we are not just friends of the One God who is the Author and ever-present Empowerer of it all, but enlightened participants in God's essential being.

As Dr. Dean Ornish puts it in *Reversing Heart Disease,* "This is not just philosophy or mysticism, for God or a higher force can be experienced. By quieting down and removing the disturbances in our mind, we can experience the underlying unity of all creation. And when we do, we can fully enjoy the richness and diversity of life in all its manifestations."[10]

Ornish, quoting various sacred texts, goes on to add that the idea of our own divinity can be realized by us because it is realized already. That is to say, it is already there; we simply need to be "awakened" to it or "to see the light." In other words, cosmic consciousness – a profoundly mystical awakening to that supreme reality described in extraordinarily similar ways by the founders of the great world religions, and by saints, prophets and gurus down the ages – is within the capacity and reach of everyone of us. With cosmic consciousness as humanity's acknowledged and globally experienced birthright, and therefore with and through fervent universal prayer in its myriad different forms, our ultimate destiny as a species can and will be realized.

As Evelyn Underhill put it in her benchmark 1974 book called *Mysticism,* "...to be a mystic is simply to participate here and now in that real and eternal life; in the fullest, deepest sense which is possible...the mystic act of union, that joyous loss of the transfigured self in God, which is the crown of man's [sic] conscious ascent toward the Absolute, is the contribution of the individual to...the destiny of the cosmos."[11]

PROBLEMS AND FURTHER QUESTIONS

Since it could be a realistic plan to write a follow-up book on this central subject (depending, of course, upon the range and depth of the response to this volume), I'm going to do something here I have never done before. I'd like to ask any of you who have a specific concern regarding prayer which was either not addressed here or was treated in either a puzzling or, in your opinion, an inadequate manner, to write or e-mail me c/o the publisher setting out your questions or comments as concisely as possible. In all likelihood, I will be unable to answer all the detailed responses personally. However, be assured that whatever you write will be read by me and responded to in any "sequel" – hopefully in the not-too-distant future. If you would not want to have your name used in such a publication, please say so clearly at some point. Your wishes will be respected and followed. The address is: c/o Northstone Publishing Inc., 9025 Jim Bailey Road, Kelowna, BC V4V 1R2 Canada. Please be brief and please mark the outside of the envelope with the word: "Prayer." If you are using the Internet, you may use either the website address http://www.prayer.joinhands.com or e-mail address tomharpur@joinhands.com.

A FINAL PRAYER OF BLESSING

Unto God's gracious mercy and protection we commit you.
May the Lord bless you and keep you and those you love.
May the Lord's face shine upon you.
May the Lord give to you and all those for whom you pray the
priceless gift of peace.
May you and yours ever be channels of light and peace to others
in this beautiful, yet suffering and environmentally degraded world.

Based upon the Aaronic blessing in Numbers 6:24–26

ACKNOWLEDGMENTS

Veteran authors know that listing their acknowledgments can be the most difficult, and even dangerous, part of writing a book. Inevitably, someone, or some place, influence, trend or event gets overlooked. I know that in writing this particular book I have been conscious of how incredibly indebted we all are to such a wide web of friends, mentors, books old and new, and ultimately to the Author of the stunning miracle of life itself. In this deeper sense, this book has been a gift to me from the Universe, and I acknowledge that with profound gratitude.

Unfortunately, it seems a clichéd formula to express thanks to one's wife "without whose patience, advice, general saintliness or whatever, this book could not have been written." But it would be deceptive to say otherwise here. Ever since we became man and wife in 1980, Susan has been a vital part of all my writing. In fact, this is the 14th book (out of a total of 15) that we have seen come to birth together. I value her inspiration, encouragement, and her invaluable care in shaping the final manuscript, more than can ever be fully said.

Thanks to the members of "The Seekers" – a small group of authors and thinkers who meet monthly at the University of Toronto Faculty Club pub to discuss works-in-progress – for their warm support and helpful suggestions.The group includes Joel Whitton, M.D., Ph.D.; Adam Crabtree, Ph.D.; novelist Sylvia Fraser; writer Joe Fisher; and several other very bright minds.

Once again I am grateful to the large company of readers of my Sunday columns in *The Toronto Star* and the viewers of my work on Vision/TV and elsewhere, for their constant feedback, questions, observations, and complaints. In this and in all my books this has kept me feeling grounded and alert to what people are feeling and thinking in "the real world" beyond theology and ideas alone.

Thanks finally to my chief editor, Mike Schwartzentruber, and everyone else at Northstone Publishing. His and their en-thusiasm for the book from the very moment we first discussed it have been tremendous. Mike's shrewd editorial suggestions and kindly criticisms where necessary produced a most creative dialogue between us and, in the end, a work about which, I believe, we can all justifiably feel happy.

PERMISSIONS

FOOTNOTES

EPIGRAPH

[1]   Here is the complete text of James Montgomery's well-known hymn on prayer as published in the Anglican hymnal (the old "blue book") used for so many years before the publication of the joint Anglican/United Church hymnal – the "red book" – in the mid-1970s.

It was listed as #438 on page 441 and was first written in 1818.

Prayer is the soul's sincere desire,
Uttered or unexpressed;
The motion of a hidden fire,
That trembles in the breast.

Prayer is the burden of a sigh,
The falling of a tear,
The upward glancing of an eye,
When none but God is near.

238 ← PRAYER:THE HIDDEN FIRE

Prayer is the simplest form of speech
That infant lips can try,
Prayer the sublimest strains that reach
The Majesty on high.

Prayer is the Christian's vital breath,
The Christian's native air,
His watchword at the gates of death:
He enters heaven with prayer.

Prayer is the contrite sinner's voice,
Returning from his ways;
While angels in their song rejoice,
And cry, "Behold, he prays."

O thou by whom we come to God,
The Life, the Truth, the Way,
The path of prayer thyself hast trod:
Lord, teach us how to pray.

INTRODUCTION

[1] Books by Larry Dossey include *Healing Words* (San Francisco: HarperSanFrancisco, 1994) and *Prayer is Good Medicine* (San Francisco: HarperSanFrancisco, 1996).

[2] Sir John Templeton, the man who pioneered mutual funds, making a vast fortune in the process, has retired from business to devote himself entirely to the investigation and promotion of the spiritual dimensions of life. The sponsor of The Templeton Prize for Progress in Religion, the world's richest prize, has now mobilized a team of 30 or more researchers to set up

a long-term strategy to discover more about the physiology of spiritual experience and the neurology of healing prayers.

At Harvard, Dr. Herbert Benson is currently expanding his staff of 35 researchers and technicians. He and his team are preparing for the systematic development of spiritual tools to heal common ailments and to ease pain. Benson and cardiologist Marianne Legato, of Columbia University's medical school now meet every six months with a network of 75 scientists to design new experiments on the puzzles of the soul. See: *Spirituality and Health Magazine*, Fall, 1996, p.3 ff.

[3]   Dr. Daniel P. Sulmasy is a Franciscan friar, a doctor, and director of the Center for Clinical Bioethics at Georgetown University Medical Center, Washington, D.C. His book is *The Healer's Calling: A Spirituality for Physicians and Other Health Care Professionals* (Mahwah, N.J.: Paulist Press, 1997), p.85.

[4]   All quotations from the Bible are from the *New Revised Standard Version*, 1989, except where otherwise specifically indicated.

[5]   Sister Wendy Beckitt, *The Mystery of Love* (New York: HarperSanFrancisco, 1996), p. ix.

CHAPTER 1: WHY PRAY?

[1]   For a discussion of the reasons for and against belief in God, see my book *Would You Believe?* (Toronto: McClelland and Stewart, 1996). The American edition, entitled *The Thinking Person's Guide to God*, was published in 1996 by Prima Press, Rocklin, California.

[2]   Dr. Herbert Benson, *Timeless Healing* (New York: Fireside Press, 1997).

[3]   James Redfield, *The Celestine Prophecy* (New York: Time Warner Books, 1994).

[4]   Tulku Thondup, *The Healing Power of Mind: Simple Exercises for Health, Well-Being, and Enlightenment* (Boston: Shambhala Publications, 1996).

[5]   Dr. Jon Kabat-Zinn, *Wherever You Go, There You Are: Mindfulness Meditation in Everyday Life* (New York: Hyperion Press, 1994).

6   Dr. David Larson, adjunct professor of psychiatry associated with Duke University Medical Center and Northwestern University Medical School, as well as president of the National Institute for Healthcare Research, has gone on record saying that doctors seldom ask patients the most important questions about their health, that is, about their spirituality. His research over many years has convinced him, for example, that whether or not a patient prays significantly affects their prognosis and rate of being healed. He has the data to back this up. See *Spirituality & Health Magazine*, Fall, 1996, p.4 and p.26.

CHAPTER 2: A CASE STUDY

1   The entire *Life After Death* series came out in a French Canadian translation early in 1997 and, later that same year, helped launch a new Quebec francophone life channel based in Montreal. It was such a success there they decided to do a rerun within weeks of the first broadcast.

2   I decided to drop this regular Sunday feature in mid-February 1997 to have more time for this book – and hopefully others to come. Helping with this decision was the realization that I would soon also be working on the production of a six-part television series based on my book on healing, *The Uncommon Touch* (Toronto: McClelland & Stewart Inc., 1991).

I am now back writing regular Sunday columns as of February 15, 1998.

3   Dr. Dean Ornish, *Reversing Heart Disease* (New York: Ballantine Books, 1990).

4   I strongly recommend the Ornish four-point program to anyone facing heart disease of any degree as well as for those keen on preventing it in the first place. The program promotes a vegetarian, low-fat diet; stress reduction through yoga and meditation; sharing of one's feelings (as opposed to mere thoughts) with a support group; and regular exercise. It not only serves your heart; my experience has convinced me one's whole life will feel and be better.

[5] "Doctor's Weigh Religion" in *Maclean's*, December 1, 1997, p.69. *The Medical Post*, which does an annual poll of doctors, was the basis for some of the *Maclean's* research. It said that 74 percent of Canadians regularly practice prayer.

CHAPTER 3: PRAYING THE LORD'S PRAYER

[1] Simone Weil, *Waiting Upon God* (New York: G. P. Putnam, 1951).

[2] *The Oxford Book of Prayer* (Oxford University Press, 1985).

[3] See *The Oxford Book of Prayer*, #842, p.277, for a slightly different version.

[4] F. W. Beare, *The Gospel According to Matthew* (New York: Harper and Row, 1981), p. 172. Subsequent references to this volume will be followed by a page number in parentheses.

CHAPTER 4: THE GOD WITHIN

[1] Jeffrey Moses, *Oneness: Great Principles Shared by All Religions* (New York: Ballantine Books, 1989).

CHAPTER 5: INNER PRAYER AND MEDITATION

[1] Jon Kabat-Zinn, *Wherever You Go, There You Are.*

[2] Benson, *Timeless Healing.*

CHAPTER 7: PRAYERS FOR PERSONAL ADAPTATION

[1] J. Carden, "An African Canticle," from *Morning, Noon and Night* (London: Church Mission Society, 1976), p. 47-48, and as quoted in *The Oxford Book of Prayer* (New York: Oxford University Press, 1985).

2   *The Toronto Sunday Star,* January 5, 1997.

3   Swami Radha's books are published by Timeless Books, PO Box 3543, Spokane, WA 99220-3543, U.S.A., Toll-free number 1-800-661-8711.

4   Swami Sivananda Radha, *The Divine Light Invocation* (Spokane, WA:Timeless Books, 1990).

CHAPTER 8: PRAYERS OF PRAISE

1   Please see my book *Would You Believe?*, where prayer as "intimate conversation" is discussed in a fuller way.

2   See the importance of the pineal gland for melatonin production and regulation *vis-à-vis* sleep, the circadian rhythm, and our various moods in Russell J. Reiter and Jo Robinson, *Melatonin: Breakthrough Discoveries That Can Help You Combat Aging, Boost Your Immune System* (New York: Bantam Books, 1995).

3   Compare Isaiah 1:10–17: "I can not endure your solemn assemblies with iniquity. Your appointed festivals my soul hates..."

4   *The Book of Common Prayer* (Toronto:Anglican Book Center,1962), p.14.

CHAPTER 9: KEEPING A PRAYER DIARY

1   In early September, 1997, she had to enter the nursing home in the Village of Lion's Head some 30 miles south of Tobermory. After she had suffered a series of falls, such as the one described here, and we had tried to keep her independence through professional daycare, we and she realized the time had come for full-time residence in a therapeutic environment. She is still in good health for her age and Susan and I were able to take her to church on Thanksgiving Sunday on October 12, 1997, just two days before I wrote this note.

Addendum: Sad to say, that was not the end of the story. Mum's condition – caused basically by simple old age, as an autopsy later revealed –

continued to deteriorate. She became confined to bed, it became more and more difficult for her to communicate with family and friends, although her mind remained bright and unimpaired.

In late November, she got a bad chest infection and died very peacefully on December 2 at 11 a.m. Fortunately, my brother, who had been her supervising doctor, and both my sisters were there with Mum – as was I – when she finally drew her last breath.

Her interment, at which I presided, was on December 6. It seemed ironic to be reading the words of the Anglican committal service at her graveside on that date because it had been set for a big community party/ reception in honor of her approaching 90th birthday(December 16). God obviously had planned for her to "party" on another plane of being altogether. May God bless her and keep her forever. Amen.

CHAPTER 10: WRESTLING WITH GOD

[1]   Richard Elliott Friedman, *The Hidden Face of God* (San Francisco: HarperSanFrancisco, 1995), p. 12.

CHAPTER 11: THE ULTIMATE GOAL OF PRAYER

[1]   Jeffrey Moses, *Oneness: Great Principles Shared by all Religions*.

[2]   Alan Cohen, *The Dragon Doesn't Live Here Anymore* (New York: Ballantine Books, 1981), p.52.

[3]   See the chapter entitled "Cosmic Consciousness" in my book *Would You Believe?*

[4]   1 Corinthians 15:28 is a key verse in the formation of my own Christology or understanding of who Jesus was and is.

[5]   *Unity Magazine,* January 1995, p.13.

6   Steven Patascher, in *Frontier Perspectives*, the learned journal of The Center for Frontier Sciences at Temple University.

7   See Paul Davies, *The Mind of God* (New York: Touchstone Books, 1993).

CHAPTER 12: KNOTS UNTIED AND CONCLUSIONS REACHED

1   Albert Einstein, *Out of My Later Years* (New York: Citadel Press, 1956).

2   Robert G. Jahn and Brenda J. Dunne, *Margins of Reality: the Role of Consciousness in the Physical World* (Orlando, FL: Harcourt Brace Jovanovich, 1987).

3   Harpur, *Would You Believe?*, pp. 66-70.

4   Daniel P. Sulmasy, *The Healer's Calling*.

5   See my section on *hypomone* or endurance in *Would You Believe?*, pp. 213-216.

6   See the introduction to *Always on Sunday* (Toronto: McClelland and Stewart, 1988).

7   See the chapter on Hinduism in *Life After Death* (Toronto: McClelland and Stewart, 1991).

8   *Would You Believe?*, pp. 184ff.

9   *How to Know God: The Yoga Aphorisms of Patanjali* (The Vedanta Society of Southern California, 1953, 1981), p.65.

10   Ornish, *Reversing Heart Disease,* pp.223-4.

11   Evelyn Underhill, *Mysticism* (New York: Meridian Books, 1974), p.447.

RECOMMENDED READING

Appleton, George, ed. *The Oxford Book of Prayer.* New York: Oxford University Press, 1985.

Bhagavad-Gita The Song of God. New York: Mentor Books, 1944.

Benor, Daniel J. *Healing Research.* Volume I. Munich: Helix Verlag, 1993.

Benson, Herbert, M.D. *Timeless Healing: The Power and Biology of Belief.* New York: Fireside Press, 1997.

Braude, Stephen E. *ESP and Psychokinesis: A Philosophical Examination.* Philadelphia: Temple University Press, 1979.

Bucke, Richard Maurice, M.D. *Cosmic Consciousness.* New York: E. P. Dutton and Co., 1969. First published in 1901 by Innes and Sons.

Chalmers, David J. "The Puzzle of Conscious Experience" in *Scientific American* 273, no. 6 (1995): 80-86.

Dossey, Larry, M.D. *Healing Words*. San Francisco: HarperSanFrancisco, 1993.

———. *Prayer is Good Medicine*. San Francisco: HarperSanFrancisco, 1996.

———. *Be Careful What You Pray For – You might just get it*. New York: HarperSanFrancisco, 1997.

———. "But Is It Energy? Reflections on Consciousness, Healing, and the New Paradigm" in *Subtle Energies 3, no. 3* (1992): 69-82.

Friedman, Richard Elliot. *The Hidden Face of God*. New York: HarperSanFrancisco, 1995.

Geissler, Eugene S., ed. *The Bible Prayer Book*. Notre Dame: Indiana, 1981.

Goswami, Amit. *The Self-Aware Universe: How Consciousness Creates the Material World*. New York: Tarcher, 1993.

Harpur, Tom. *Always on Sunday*. Toronto: Oxford University Press, 1988.

———. *Life After Death*. Toronto: McClelland & Stewart Inc., 1991.

———. *God Help Us*. Toronto: McClelland & Stewart Inc., 1992.

———. *For Christ's Sake*. New Canadian Edition. Toronto: McClelland & Stewart, 1993.

———. *The Uncommon Touch: An Investigation of Spiritual Healing*. Toronto: McClelland & Stewart Inc., 1994.

———. *Would You Believe? Finding God Without Losing Your Mind*. Toronto: McClelland & Stewart Inc., 1996. (The American edition was published as *The Thinking Person's Guide to God*. Rocklin, CA: Prima Press, 1996.)

Holy Bible. The New Revised Standard Version [NRSV] Grand Rapids, Michigan: 1989.

How to Know God, The Yoga Affirmations of Patanjali. The Vedanta Society of Southern California, 1953, 1981.

Kabat-Zinn, Jon. *Wherever You Go, There You Are: Mindfulness Meditation in Everyday Life*. New York: Hyperion Press, 1994.

———. *Full Catastrophe Living: A Practical Guide to Mindfulness, Meditation and Healing*. New York: Hyperion Press, 1991.

Lewis, C. S. *Letters to Malcolm: Chiefly on Prayer*. New York: Harcourt Brace Jovanovich, 1964.

Moses, Jeffrey. *Oneness: Great Principles Shared by all Religions*. New York: Ballantine Books, 1989.

Oxtoby, William, ed. *World Religions*. Two volumes. Toronto: Oxford University Press, 1996.

Radha, Swami Sivananda. *Time to be Holy – Reflecting on Daily Life*. Spokane: Timeless Books, 1996. Other books written by Radha and also available from Timeless Books include: *The Divine Light Invocation*; *Mantras, Words of Power; Radha, Diary of a Woman's Search; Realities of the Dreaming Mind*; and, *Kundalini Yoga for the West*. (In Canada, Timeless Books can be reached at Box 9, Kootenay Bay, BC, V0B 1X0. 1-800-661-8711).

Rein, Glen. *Quantum Biology: Healing with Subtle Energy*. Palo Alto: Quantum Biology Research Labs, 1992.
——. "The Scientific Basis for Healing with Subtle Energies." Appendix A in Leonard Laskow, *Healing with Love*, 279–319. New York: HarperCollins, 1992.

Sokoloff, Arthur. *Life Without Stress – The Far Eastern Antidote to Tension and Anxiety*. New York: Broadway Books, 1997.

Thondup, Tulku. *The Healing Power of Mind, Simple Exercises for Health, Well-Being, and Enlightenment*. Boston: Shambhala Publications Inc., 1996.

Vardey, Lucinda. *God in all Worlds*. Toronto: Alfred A. Knopf, 1995.

The Upanishads – *Breath of the Eternal*. New York: Mentor Books, 1948.

Weil, Simone. *Waiting Upon God*. New York: G. P. Putnam, 1951, also by Harper and Row, 1973.

INDEX